EXIT TEAMS

*Build a Team of Advisors
for Your Business Sale
to Get a Higher Price*

BOB TANKESLEY, MBA, CPA

EXIT TEAMS: BUILD A TEAM OF ADVISORS FOR YOUR BUSINESS SALE TO GET A HIGHER PRICE

Copyright 2024 Bob Tankesley, MBA, CPA

This work is licensed under a Creative Common Attribution-Noncommercial-NoDerivative Works 3.0 Unported License.

Attribution – You must attribute the work in the manner specified by the author or licensor (but not in any way that suggests that they endorse you or your use of the work).

Noncommercial – You may not use this work for commercial purposes.

No Derivative Works – You may not alter, transform, or build upon this work.

Inquiries about additional permissions should be directed to Bob Tankesley

Paperback Print ISBN 979-8-9918193-0-5

Hardback Print ISBN 979-8-9918193-1-2

Library of Congress Control Number – xxxxxxxxxx

Cover Design by Matt Kunz w/ the help of www.canva.com

The stories in this book are historical, personal, or fictitious. The names of well-known persons may be included. Personal stories, references, and general information are from various sources based on research and interpretation. Names and specific organizations are included where it is relevant.

Fictitious stories are included as they are similar to events and activities that happened in the past as well as in present times. Any semblance of or relation to real people is entirely coincidental.

DEDICATION

To all those risk-takers with the courage to invent the American Dream. May you achieve the success you've always wanted.

TABLE of CONTENTS

1. INTRODUCTION   1
2. DAY 1 WEDNESDAY   4
   7:55 A.M.
3. DAY 1 WEDNESDAY   10
   9:10 A.M.
4. DAY 1 WEDNESDAY   14
   9:35 A.M.
5. DAY 1 WEDNESDAY   19
   2:20 P.M.
6. DAY 1 WEDNESDAY   23
   3:25 P.M.
7. DAY 1 WEDNESDAY   27
   4:05 P.M.
8. DAY 1 WEDNESDAY   32
   4:50 P.M.
9. DAY 2 THURSDAY   40
   8:15 A.M.

10.	DAY 2 THURSDAY 12:55 P.M.	47
11.	DAY 2 THURSDAY 2:05 P.M.	55
12.	DAY 2 THURSDAY 2:15 P.M.	60
13.	DAY 2 THURSDAY 3:00 P.M.	65
14.	DAY 2 THURSDAY 4:00 P.M.	72
15.	DAY 3 FRIDAY 8:35 A.M.	78
16.	DAY 4 SATURDAY 7:00 P.M.	84
17.	DAY 6 MONDAY 8:15 A.M.	91
18.	DAY 7 TUESDAY 10:15 A.M.	97
19.	DAY 8 WEDNESDAY 6:30 P.M.	105
20.	DAY 9 THURSDAY 8:05 A.M.	115
21.	DAY 10 FRIDAY 3:30 P.M.	121

22.	DAY 13 MONDAY 7:45 A.M.	128
23.	DAY 14 TUESDAY 6:30 P.M.	135
24.	DAY 15 WEDNESDAY 9:00 A.M.	141
25.	DAY 15 WEDNESDAY 9:35 A.M.	147
26.	DAY 15 WEDNESDAY 6:15 P.M.	152
27.	DAY 16 THURSDAY 8:40 A.M.	158
28.	DAY 16 THURSDAY 3:25 P.M.	165
29.	DAY 16 THURSDAY 5:45 P.M.	170
30.	DAY 17 FRIDAY 7:35 A.M.	176
31.	DAY 17 FRIDAY 9:10 A.M.	188
32.	DAY 20 MONDAY 10:50 A.M.	195
33.	DAY 34 MONDAY 6:00 A.M.	200

34.	DAY 62 MONDAY 9:15 A.M.	208
35.	DAY 63 TUESDAY 8:58 A.M.	214
36.	DAY 90 MONDAY 10:40 A.M.	220
37.	DAY 174 MONDAY 2:35 P.M.	227
38.	DAY 258 MONDAY SUNSET	234
39.	CONCLUSION	239
40.	TRAINING CAMP	241
41.	A CLOSER LOOK INDEX	243
42.	ACKNOWLEDGEMENTS	247
43.	ABOUT THE AUTHOR	249

1
INTRODUCTION

Living the American Dream is full of excitement. Businesses open daily with the owner's dreams of personal and monetary fulfillment. Hard-working business owners strive for freedom, working with their hands and minds to build systems and processes that serve their markets and reap the rewards. Owning a business is one of the grandest adventures a person can undertake.

Owning a business is not without its risk. With the rewards so high, the competition is fierce. The market is fickle. Things change on a dime. The path to freedom is through the galleys of work. Many don't endure, and too many businesses in America ultimately fail.

Those who do endure, however, figure out their systems. They establish their cash flow, the lifeblood of their business. They experience success and reap some rewards. As they age, they see the light at the end of the tunnel. It's the light of freedom, and time is rushing them toward it.

Then, suddenly, the business owner realizes it's not freedom. It's a train. It's market changes or competitors or customers or health concerns. Circumstances have added to the pressure right when he hopes to be unburdened. The risk has grown stronger with the advent of time. To find his freedom, he must survive the threats. Those threats are often external. But the primary threat comes from within himself. He's a fighter, fighting for freedom and control. After all, that's why he owned a business. This time, however, his opposition knows this. When he tries to sell his business buyers will prey on his psychology. With the pressure mounting, he risks falling into a trap, never to find the freedom he imagined.

After over a decade of assisting business sellers, I've seen this scenario play out over and over again. For every business seller I've helped, there are countless others who, for one reason or another, decided to charge on their own headlong into the light, only to be run over at the closing.

I wrote this book to reach business owners before they decide to sell or, if they are in the process of selling, to consider a different approach other than the one that first attracted them, before disaster strikes. This is not a "One-Size-Fits-All How to Sell Your Business" book. Every business is unique in the marketplace, and each business transaction is a game of its own, comprising two teams negotiating against each other for the best deal. A "One-Size-Fits-All How to Sell Your Business" book might educate you on certain tactics, but it won't give you the feeling of what it's like to use them at the right time and in the right circumstance.

Rather, I wanted to write a book that gives you, the Reader, an experience. I wanted you to go through a business sale, imagining yourself as a business owner suddenly feeling the increased pressures and navigating the choices and stresses of running a business while considering a sale. I wanted you to understand the characters who will influence you, who will pressure you, who will mislead you, and who will help you. I wanted you to watch how hopes and dreams grow, die, and become realized through the business selling process. I wanted you to feel the threats, the choices, the pressures, the defeats, and the wins through this story before you have to face them in real life.

Purchasing and reading this book will be far less costly and far less risky than leaving millions on the table during an unsuccessful closing. My hope is you take the time to read Exit Teams and, when finished, you absorb the story. Exit Teams will inspire you to change both your approach and your business so you might maximize your opportunities rather than regret what you left on the table. Let it guide you today as you build your business. Then, one day, your business will fly on its own while affording you your hopes and dreams in retirement.

2
DAY 1 WEDNESDAY
7:55 A.M.

Dave put his breakfast tray on the table. The business owners gathered around circular tables, chatting and passing out business cards. A speaker approached the podium, announcing they'd start the meeting in a few minutes. After he sat down, Dave enjoyed his eggs and bacon while listening to the other business owners. He had a knack for listening. He often picked up tips he might implement that day to help his bottom line. It's one of the things that made him successful.

Dr. Cal White, a dentist, sat to Dave's left. Dave had sent his family to Dr. White's dental practice over the years, where Cal had cleaned Dave's and his wife's teeth. "How's business?" Cal said.

"Good," Dave said. "Paying the bills."

Cal chuckled. "I see that big truck you have out there. Looks like you're doing more than paying the bills."

"Guilty pleasure," Dave said. He picked up a piece of bacon and chewed, trying not to smile.

"And you've got quite a tan. Did you get back from the beach?"

Dave swallowed. "Yeah. Kathy and I just returned from Destin."

"Rental?"

"No. We've got a condo and a boat down there. Comes in handy when we entertain clients."

"Nice," Cal said.

Across the table, Allison engaged with Patti in a conversation about artificial intelligence. Allison owned a marketing company and was proud of it. Dave liked sitting next to Allison because she was knowledgeable about new marketing technology.

Bert Muncey approached the table across from Dr. White. A real estate closing attorney with political aspirations, he sat down, smiled, and shook hands with those around him before a member from another table tapped him on the shoulder, inviting him to be introduced to one of the guests.

Dave enjoyed these breakfasts. There were many important people there, people with aspirations and goals. These people were in control of their businesses, just like he was. They were the movers and the shakers. He liked being one of them. As Dave bit into another strip of bacon, Mark Bragowski's tray clanked on the other side of the table. The man grinned, folding his sunglasses and showing the white pearly teeth that the dentist gave him. "You look happy," Cal said.

"I am." Mark sat down and leaned back into his chair. As Dave studied him, he couldn't tell if Mark acted more like a man about to sail on a pontoon boat or a man who just conquered the mountain and claimed himself as king.

"Why so happy?" Dave said.

Before Mark opened his mouth, Bill Walters walked behind him and slapped him on the shoulders. "I hear congratulations are in order!"

"News travels fast," Mark said.

"What news?" Dave wondered. Mark and Dave had been friends for decades. They had attended these breakfasts, and each time it was the same. Mark and Dave would chat with the other business owners, have their breakfast, listen to the program, and they'd compare notes once all that was finished. Dave always tried to bring something of value to share with Mark, and Mark had always brought something for Dave to use in his business. Today, however, was different. Mark was happy; too happy. If Mark was happy, then it had to be about business. It must have been good if Mark had found a new tactic or strategy for his business. Dave couldn't wait to hear the tactic and initiate it in his own business.

Dave said, "What's he congratulating you about?"

Bragowski leaned forward, his hands on the table. He grinned at the people at the table. "Well, boys. I'm selling."

Dave swallowed.

"You are?" Cal said. "I thought you loved textiles."

"I do. But when New York comes callin', it's not a bad idea to listen." Bragowski held his head high like he had won the lottery.

Dave put his bacon on the plate.

"They made you a good offer?" Allison said, as though she could read the pride in Bragowski's face.

"It's tempting," he said. Humility was not Bragowski's strong suit.

A flash of wonder went through Dave's mind. Several decades ago, he and Bragowski had begun their businesses within three months of each other in the same industrial park. Bragowski was in textiles, and Dave was in manufacturing. They had met a few weeks after and struck up a friendship. Their families grew alongside each other, and their sons played on the Giants T-Ball team at the local park.

Now their kids were out of school and living their own lives. Even though the expenses from the college tuition, weddings, and grandchildren added up, that didn't stop them from buying their bi-annual four-door trucks at the Atlanta dealership. They had scheduled their joint family spring break trips, including a fishing excursion in the Keys.

Bragowski's selling, however, made Dave pause. His own business paid for everything, and he knew Bragoski's business did the same. Why, then, would he sell? Was it age? They were both in their late sixties, but Dave felt he had at least ten more years. Mark never hinted once about selling. Health didn't seem to be an issue. The New York firm must have made an incredible offer.

"I'm surprised," Dave said. "Congratulations. You've made it."

"Come on over this afternoon," Bragowski said. "I'll tell you about it."

"Can't. Doctor's appointment."

"You alright?"

"Yeah. Just routine checkup." Dave leaned back. "But tomorrow works."

The president of the business club stepped to the podium and hammered the gavel, starting the meeting.

"Come by at three," Bragowski said.

Dave nodded as the President asked everyone to stand.

A CLOSER LOOK

Our hero, Dave, has owned his business for several years and hadn't thought of selling for good reason: the business paid his mortgage, his wife's expenses, his family vacations, his kids' college expenses, and the new highly-customized pickup truck he bought every other year. After all, Bragowski kept buying trucks. Dave would not let himself be outdone when they parked next to each other at the morning business socials.

His wife, Kathy, often shopped with Bragowski's wife, Melissa. When they had their shopping excursions, Kathy compared their lifestyles, telling Dave how he should spend his money so they wouldn't be outdone. Dave didn't mind. He liked competing. Even though he and Bragowski had their ups and downs, he knew if he maintained his positive mindset things would work in his favor.

But this was different. Selling was a big step, one he hadn't considered. He wanted to wait until after he met with Bragowski before telling Kathy.

DECISION

After the meeting, Dave circled the table while Mark stood. "So how'd it all go down?"

Mark grinned. "Right place, right time. Got a phone call. They came to town, and we shook hands."

"That was it?"

"Well, the deal isn't signed yet, but Melissa's excited. I figure if it makes her this happy, might as well take the plunge."

"But, you love your business. What are you going to do?"

"I'll come up with something. Don't you worry about me. Come on over tomorrow and I'll give you more info."

Dave nodded, and they shook hands. As Mark skipped out of the breakfast hall, Dave's foot kicked a chair leg. Frustrated at Mark's victory, one that Dave would never be able to top unless he sold his own business, he went to his truck. As he turned the ignition, he shook his head. "Better blow off steam first," he said as he turned the steering wheel and exited the parking lot.

3
DAY 1 WEDNESDAY
9:10 A.M.

Dave sat at the bench press. Nothing like a few sets of reps to get the stress out, he thought. He gripped the bar, lifted it off the rack, and lowered it to his chest. His skin felt tight from his suntan. His breathing was off. He held his breath, trying to recover his rhythm. He pressed his arms, but the bar was too heavy. His face turned red. He didn't want to ask for help. The last thing he needed was for the gym's young up-and-comers to feel sorry for him. But he pressed, and his air wasn't working. He was too uptight over the news about Mark. What will happen when Melissa tells Kathy? He'll hear it at home. If he doesn't keep up with Mark, Kathy will find a way to get under his skin. She always did.

He pressed again. He heard himself grunting. He lifted the bar two inches, held it for three seconds, and lowered it to his chest.

"Hey old man. You need help?" A young trainer came over and placed his hands above the bar.

"I got it," Dave said.

"Okay." The young man stepped back but kept his eyes on him.

Dave pressed again. He lifted the bar four inches this time, then five, but it stalled.

"Here," the trainer said.

Dave nodded, his face red.

The young trainer lifted the bar with one hand and set it down on the rack. The bar banged against the rack as it hit metal on metal. "That's a pretty heavy warmup."

Dave blew the air out of his lungs. He sat up and leaned forward, his lungs inhaling and exhaling. "Too much, too soon?"

"If you need help, here's my card."

Dave took the card. "Thanks, but I'm just having an off day."

"No problem. For thirty dollars for half-an-hour, I'll make sure that doesn't happen to you again. In this line of work, a little help goes a long way. And hiring someone else to help you can get you to your goal more quickly."

Dave pressed his lips together. He never liked paying someone when he should do it himself. "No thanks," he said. I've got it all under control."

The young man winked. "If those weights say differently, let me know." He walked between the equipment to the other side of the room.

"Cocky son-of-a...," Dave mumbled. As the trainer moved to help a young woman at the free weights, Dave stood up and went to a machine. He sat down and put the pin in the plate. Too heavy, he thought. He pulled the pin out and reduced the weight. He pushed the grip back and forth, feeling his muscles flex and release, his lungs expand and contract. His shock about Mark turned into anger about himself.

A CLOSER LOOK

Business is a competitive game. One's standing and reputation among peers can drive emotions, decisions, and actions. When a business owner gets the idea of selling, whether it originates from his own needs or that of a colleague, the mere anticipation of it can affect his mindset and add stress. The business owner feels this stress because he is not as young as he used to be. He may be battle-hardened through the years of competition, but his age now burdened his thoughts and emotions. These questions - whether factual or imagined - exist because of anticipated change. They will flood his mind with thoughts, expectations, scenarios, doubts, and fears. They can cause his mind to become distracted or forgetful.

Remember, too, that most business owners in the process of selling are slightly older than normal retirement age, which ranges from 62 to 67 years old. Thus, not only can the stress of selling a business during his advanced years affect him mentally, but it can affect him physically, too. The physical symptoms include rapid breathing, lack of coordination, reduced energy levels, etc.

As he thinks about the challenge of selling his business, figuring out his cash flow, managing home expenses, announcing the change to his family, and deciding what he will do for the rest of his life, his day-to-day behavior may change. Whether he realizes it or not, the prospect of selling, if unprepared, can leave him personally and professionally vulnerable.

DECISION

Feeling better about blowing off steam, Dave showered in the locker room and dressed. As he was leaving, a middle-aged woman tried to work the machine he had just left, but she did not understand it.

   He walked up to her while she held the pin in her hand.

   "May I?" he said.

   "I'm not sure how this thing works."

   "Here." He pointed to the place to put the pin. "Now grip here." She held her hands on the bar. "Now push, but do it slow. Keep the elbows inside."

   "Oh. Thanks!"

   "If you need any further help, that trainer over there can assist you."

   She nodded and said "Thank you." Then she pushed the weights, her arms moving back and forth.

   Dave threw his gym bag over his shoulder and left the building.

4
DAY 1 WEDNESDAY
9:35 A.M.

Dave pulled his truck into the FineLine Manufacturing parking lot. The lights in the windows were on, which normally gave him a comforting feeling because it was always good to see that the lights were on. Except this time he imagined the windows being dark. If he sold, who would keep the lights on? Would they remain open? What would happen to his customers? What would happen to his employees? What would happen to his family?

What would happen to him?

He took a deep breath. "The lights are on today," he said. "Let's get to work."

He walked through the front doors, sticking his chest out and telling himself he was in control. His receptionist, Ava, sat at her desk and talked with a caller on the phone. She waved hello while speaking into the headset. Dave tapped her desk with his finger and mouthed, "Any calls?" She nodded and pointed behind her towards accounting. It had to be Diane. She was the one who took calls when he wasn't there.

Dave said hello to a few of his employees and approached Diane. Before he could say anything, she said, "There was a

Mr. Steele who called for you. Didn't leave his business name or phone number, though. Said he'd call back."

"Sales call?"

"Aren't they all?"

Dave grinned. "Thanks. Where's Tim?"

"In the back. CWB called in a good-sized order. He's helping in the warehouse."

Dave thanked her and went through the back doors, imagining a would-be buyer drooling over his smoothly-run operation. The familiar scent of cardboard, grease, and chemicals filled his nostrils. The smell of production, he thought.

As the doors swung open, however, he heard the sounds of men shouting. Between the high rows of shelves, Tim picked up a loose box off the concrete while motioning with his head. "Get those off the floor. We have to get this order rewrapped!" The four other men bent down and started moving boxes.

Dave's first reaction was to scan the room and confirm nobody from OSHA was on site for an inspection. "What the hell happened?" Dave said.

Tim raised his eyes. His face was red. "The wrapping snapped, and the boxes fell off the pallet." The men paused when they realized Dave was there. "Why are you stopping?" Tim said. "Get to work!" The men snapped to attention and resumed stacking the boxes on the pallet.

"Is this the CWB order?" Dave said.

"Yes, sir."

Dave raised his arm. "Ok. Tim, get these guys to rewrap the pallet, then meet me in my office."

"Yes, sir. Should I bring Cliff with me?"

"Why?"

"Manufacturing wraps the pallets for CWB."

Dave nodded. "Yes. Bring him." He huffed as he went back through the warehouse doors into the main office.

A CLOSER LOOK

Dave is like most business owners. He got into business to work for himself, keep his schedule, and make his own decisions. He worked nights and weekends. Eventually, he hired employees, gained more customers, and his business realized more income. He was able to increase his salary, buy his family a bigger home, and take some better vacations.

But he still had to manage his business. If he went away too long, he'd return and find unexpected problems. Small problems grew into big ones, and upon his return not only did he have to take care of the big problems first, but he never seemed to be able to get the small problems worked out to their completion. He ran as fast as he could, but now at his age, he would only go until he felt burnout creeping in. At that point, he'd adopt his business owner privileges and take off for the afternoon, never quite completing the systems he depended upon to give him those privileges.

A business with an absent business owner can experience multiple problems if his systems aren't there to support it. In Dave's case, it's a bad sign when his team has trouble fulfilling a large sales order. It's a worse sign if he doesn't know who handles a portion of his various business processes. If these problems exist during a business sale, it will only spell disaster for the business owner, his family, and his financial future.

DECISION

Dave stood in front of the large conference table. He held a marker and made himself ready to write on the whiteboard.

Tim and Cliff walked into the office, their eyes wide ready for a tongue-lashing.

Dave said, "Guys, what's going on back there?"

Tim said, "Bad wrapping."

Cliff said, "I can explain…"

"Who did it?" Dave interrupted.

"Peter, but that's not–"

"Were you supervising him?"

"I was bu–"

"Dammit, Cliff. This is a big order!"

Cliff closed his mouth.

Tim leaned forward. "Sir, it wasn't the wrapper."

"What do you mean?"

"Peter didn't do anything different. It's bad wrapping, as in bad stretch wrap. The stuff is so thin it's bound to break."

"We haven't had this problem before."

"No sir. But you told us last week to cut our packaging costs 20% across the board. We were already using the cheapest stretch wrap on the market. All we could do was wrap it 20% less."

Dave paused, remembering his manager's meeting from last week. "Did you try negotiating with the manufacturer?"

"Negotiate with the vendor who is already the cheapest? How?"

"Call another company. Get a bid."

Tim nodded. Cliff sat still, awaiting instruction.

Dave wrote the letters CWB on the whiteboard. "Okay. Go fulfill that order." Tim and Cliff left the conference room and returned to the warehouse. Dave leaned forward, put his hands on the conference table, and lowered his head.

5
DAY 1 WEDNESDAY
2:20 P.M.

Dave left the office early and climbed into his truck. His radio played AC/DC's "Thunderstruck," something to keep his spirits up, but it wasn't working. He admitted to himself that he was nervous about his doctor's visit. He had been more tired than usual, and today seemed especially hard. He thought of Kathy, his wife of forty years. They had met in college and dated on and off after school. He worked in sales for a shipping courier before he found himself in management. After his promotion, he took Kathy to her favorite restaurant on Saint Simons Island along the Georgia coast. He dropped to one knee, held up a ring, and proposed. When she said, "Yes" he felt like the luckiest man alive.

Though that was so long ago, he still cherished those memories with her. He wanted to call and talk with her. He dialed the number on his cell phone. He smiled when he heard Kathy's voice echo from the stereo speakers. "Hey, honey."

"Melissa told me that Mark is selling," Kathy said.

Dave frowned. Damn, she knows. "Really?" he said.

"Some big New York firm approached them. Offered a lot of cash. Melissa told me she and Mark are planning to sell and spend two months in Italy."

"They are?"

"Yeah. Melissa is already looking at a villa in Tuscany. We should go with them."

Dave bit his lip. Mark had him beat. And now Kathy's desire to spend money added more pressure. "Two months is a long time."

"Oh, honey. It'll be fun. You deserve a long vacation."

"We just got back from the beach."

"I know. I want to go back already."

"Let's not talk about it now," Dave said.

"It's okay," Kathy said. "Tell you what. I'll start making plans. You just have to get on the plane when I tell you."

And write the check, Dave thought.

Kathy spoke through her mental checklist, as she often did. Dave drove while she talked, trying not to worry about his doctor's visit until he pulled into the medical parking lot.

"What do you think?" Kathy said.

Dave remembered his meeting scheduled with Bragowski for tomorrow. He would have to determine quickly if he should sell or not. "Can we talk about this when I get home?"

"Are you going in a meeting?"

"Sorry. I have this doctor's checkup."

"Oh, that is today, isn't it? I'm sure you'll be fine. You're in great health. All the same, have him check that spot on your shoulder."

That's right. The spot. Dave couldn't decide whether he had forgotten about it or if he just didn't want to think about it. He made a mental note. "Will do," Dave said.

"Okay."

"What are you doing today?"

"Shopping."

Dave nodded. "Have fun."

"Love you."

"Love you too." Dave hung up the phone and stared at the large reflective glass windows of the medical building in front of him.

A CLOSER LOOK

As most business owners considering the sale of their business are in their late sixties or early seventies, navigating a potential sale has its personal and professional challenges. Just because the business owner's mind has shifted to the possibility of selling, telling his family isn't always easy. The business owner won't have all the answers to their questions. This poses a challenge. Nobody wants to present a giant change to his family without knowing the answers. But that's precisely the situation in which he'll often find himself.

A common approach is to stall and talk about other things until those answers become clear. Unfortunately, this only adds to the stress and the pressure. The prospect of selling becomes an elephant in the room, one the business owner hides until the spouse begins to wonder what's wrong.

Another approach is to talk about it only once but then not mention it again. This will cause additional problems because the spouse and family will worry about their expectations. These worries and expectations can hurt communication within relationships, which adds to the stress and makes the business owner even more vulnerable.

The situation can become especially difficult when family members suggest – or worse, demand – a seat at the negotiating table. While their involvement can be literal or figurative, pressures from family add to the complexity of change.

These pressures aren't atypical, but they are dangerous. These reactions are common in human nature as people try to navigate change. Still, without understanding common pitfalls, it's easy to find the business owner growing more and more vulnerable before his business sale.

DECISION

Dave exited his truck and inhaled. "You've got this," he said. "You're in control." He marched into the medical offices and navigated between the patients to the check-in desk.

6
DAY 1 WEDNESDAY
3:25 P.M.

Dave sat on the cold table with his shirt off. The room smelled sterile. He felt embarrassed with the hospital gown barely covering his backside. He stiffened his torso. If he sat straight, Willis and his physician's assistant, a large woman named Nina, wouldn't be able to see any more of his skin than necessary.

Doctor Willis held the clipboard in his hand, his eyes staring at the paper. Nina looked serious. Dave sensed Willis wasn't telling him something.

"You're quiet," Dave said.

"I want you to see a specialist about that spot on your shoulder," Willis said.

A shiver ran through Dave's body. "What is it?"

Willis tapped the clipboard with his pen. "Maybe nothing, but I'm old enough to have seen a lot of things. The shape and color of it is off, and it's best you get it looked at."

"Cancer?"

"Can't say. Again, it may be nothing, but let's just make sure it's not. I'll have Marge schedule you with Doctor Blackwood. He's who we recommend our patients to for skin issues. Of course, you're always free to get a second opinion."

Dave gripped the table he sat on, feeling the cold metal on his palms and fingertips. "Thanks."

Willis and Nina left the room, with Dave's heart beating inside his chest. He was in his late sixties. This morning he had a rough go at the gym. Now this? He thought of Kathy and his kids, Don and Katelyn. What would happen to his business if something happened to him? They needed that cash flow. They needed the perks that the business provided.

He remembered the smile on Bragowski's face. They were the same age. Maybe he had the right idea. Maybe it was time to look into selling his business.

A CLOSER LOOK

There are numerous reasons a business owner decides to sell, but those reasons are divided into one of two camps: personal or business. Personal reasons typically have to do with himself or his family, including health (either the business owner's or a family member's), increasing age, decreasing energy, loss of interest, mid-life crises, divorces, child custody, moving to another location, or any other number of personal reasons.

Business reasons typically have to do with some aspect of the business itself suffering, such as competitors entering the market, changing regulations (or merely the changing interpretation of those regulations by government authorities), loss of a key person, rising costs, decreasing revenue, employee turnover, and any number of other conditions that make the operating of the business less desirable.

Whatever the reason, some incident comes at the business owner that makes him consider the prospect of no longer owning his business, and then selling it to someone else. He knows this will create a significant change in his personal life. Not only will it affect the cash flow he currently enjoys, but it will also affect his very identity. If he is no longer a business owner, who is he? What will he do once he sells? Who will he become?

The newness of this prospect forces him to consider change. But the newness also makes his mind run. How exactly will he sell his business? Is it the right thing to do? Whom can he trust? At this point, several questions run through his mind and he won't know all the answers.

DECISION

Dave drove his truck, his mind wandering. He thought of Kathy and his kids. He did not want to worry them. He considered downplaying the doctor's recommendation about his shoulder. He briefly considered not telling Kathy at all, but that wouldn't be right. She needed to know.

He had to admit he was worried. Was it melanoma? Was it something worse? That spot had been there for months, yet he hadn't done anything about it. He had decided to ignore it, hoping it would go away. He was too busy managing his business, going to the gym, driving his truck, going on vacations, and taking care of Kathy. Damn, he thought. Why didn't he address it when he first noticed it?

He slammed on the brakes, narrowly running into the car in front of him. Embarrassed, he waved an apology to the driver, then he told himself to regain his composure. Worrying never works, he thought. Action is all that matters. I'm in control. Always in control.

He dialed Kathy. It went to voicemail. "Shopping," he said before the phone beeped. He projected his best positive voice. "Hi Honey. I'm out of the doctor's office. I just want to let you know they looked at that spot on my shoulder. He says it's probably nothing, but he still wants me to go see a specialist. I don't want you to worry, but I'm scheduled to see the specialist next week. Have fun with Melissa. Love you."

He hung up the phone and stared ahead at the road. His truck rolled through the quiet side streets. What would he do next? He dialed Bragowski's business number.

Terri, his secretary, answered. "Hi, Dave. He's not in right now."

"I know. I just wanted to confirm we have an appointment at three o'clock tomorrow in his office."

"That's right. It's on his calendar."

"Great. I'll see you then."

"See you then."

Dave hung up. He told himself things would work out. He could do this. He was in control. He reached for his phone and dialed his son.

7
DAY 1 WEDNESDAY
4:05 P.M.

Don answered the phone, which Dave thought surprising considering his son's rising career. Dave was proud of Don's economic growth. His son earned his B.A. in marketing from the University of Georgia, worked a few years in sales for a Fortune 500 company, and went back to school to achieve his M.B.A. at Georgia Tech. These days, Don was a rising star in the securities industry. He loved talking stocks and bonds. At thirty-eight, he married late. He and his wife would come over for holidays and special occasions, bringing the grandkids. Dave and Kathy loved the grandkids. Maybe that was his calling, Dave thought. If he sold, he could spend more time with the grandkids. Isn't that what people plan when they retire? But who would buy his business? Dave had assumed one day Don would take over the family business, but every time the holidays came around, Don grew shy about those conversations.

But with the news today about his health, Dave had to ask. "How's the market?"

"We live in interesting times, Dad. You know how it goes."

"Are you in the green?"

"Always," Don said.

"That's great," Dave said. He swallowed. It was now or never. "Don, I wanted to ask you something."

"Sure, Dad. What is it?"

"What would you think about coming to work for me?"

Silence.

"I know you've got a good thing going," Dave said. "But I also know it's stressful. If you buy the business, it can give you and your family more stability. More time. The employees respect you." Dave found it was harder to sell his son on this idea of a buyout than it was to sell a customer his products.

"You can't afford me," Don said.

The sound of his voice told Dave something else was coming. "I didn't want to tell you this until I knew for sure, but I just got an offer from Wall Street. Goldman Sachs sent a recruiter after me and I interviewed with them. I even flew up to meet with their regional director. They made me an incredible offer, and I just can't turn it down."

"That's great, son," Dave said. "Why didn't you tell me?"

"We're going to move to Connecticut."

Dave thought about the grandkids. Oh, Nellie. Kathy isn't going to like this news. The last thing Dave wanted was a depressed wife, and this news would achieve just that. Dave swallowed and said, "That's great, son. I'm proud of you."

"Thanks, Dad."

"When are you moving?"

"We're putting the house up for sale this weekend."

"Oh," Dave said. He couldn't help but think he was getting kicked in the stomach. Everything was happening so fast.

They talked about the markets, the Fed, the government, and commodities. Dave didn't mention the doctor's appointment. He didn't want to take away from his son's opportunity. It was a reason to celebrate. Dave told Don that they'd throw one of their famous outdoor parties - fully catered, of course. Kathy would make sure of that.

They hung up the phone. As Dave drove along the streets, he put his hands to his mouth. He thought of his daughter, Katelyn. She was an artist in Savannah. She worked for a company doing graphic design. She could buy the business, but never in all her years had she shown the slightest inclination of interest. He chuckled. "Too much like her mother," he said. Then he bit his lip. What was he going to do now?

A CLOSER LOOK

A family member (or key employee) is what business buyers and sellers refer to as an inside buyer. The typical inside buyer the business owner approaches first is a family member, and if not one, perhaps another. Usually, the priority is that the business remains in the family, and the business owner goes down the list of family members and explores every possible buyer. After all, it was a cash-generating system that provided for them all these years. It makes sense to keep a good thing going.

If the owner is considering an inside buyer, the owner and the buyer engage in a series of conversations, usually over a couple of years. Thus, the business owner is preparing the inside buyer for the transition that will help the business remain stable while keeping the annuity checks flowing for the seller.

Of course, the family members may opt-out. They can refuse for a number of reasons: lack of interest in what the business does, other opportunities, changing markets, geography, locale, and relationships. The business owner could try to sell his family member on purchasing the business, and he may be successful, but the family member, whether he understands it or not, is now a potential buyer with the right to refuse. If he says, "No," family relationships change, and the business owner feels more stress while he seeks another answer.

When an inside buyer is a family member, the planning and preparation is less haphazard. But what happens when there is no family member or key employee? That's when things become far more difficult.

DECISION

Dave thinks about all that's happened today. He expected today to be another win, working to build his business, beat Mark Bragowski, and then go home to Kathy. Instead, he's suddenly thinking about selling his business, he's got issues in the warehouse, and he has to see a cancer specialist. Without a doubt, these events threw him off his game today. But he had overcome days like this. In thirty years of business, he had seen a lot. He had survived a lot. This was a strange day, but he reminded himself he was in control. He could come back swinging tomorrow and still win the week. It was time to get his focus back on his business.

He shook his head. "Concentrate, Dave," he said. Losing focus wasn't like him. He loved his business. He had to get back in the groove. That's what he needed right now. Bragowski's selling and the doctor's news caused him to flinch. But he wasn't a flincher. He was a competitor. He had won in the past and he was going to win again!

Already thinking of a new plan, he turned his steering wheel and drove his truck toward home.

8
DAY 1 WEDNESDAY
4:50 P.M.

He pulled into the driveway of his large home. Kathy's car was in the garage. He walked into the kitchen. Kathy's purse sat on the bar but she wasn't in sight. Bernie, his giant Saint Bernard, lumbered up to him, his long tongue sliding out of the side of his mouth. Dave patted the large dog on his head. "Good boy. Where's your mom?"

Bernie glanced toward the ceiling.

"I'm up here!" Kathy shouted from the upstairs bedroom.

Dave went into his office. Papers and folders covered his oak desk. On the top were his quarterly investment statements from Richard Momoney, his financial advisor. He needed to call him, he thought. He pushed the paper aside to clear an area for him to write. A picture of him, Kathy, and his kids sat on his desk. It was the one they took on the beach twenty years ago. His hair was less gray, Kathy was smiling, Don was thinner, and Katelyn still had braces. Behind the picture, a shelf held several books whose titles referenced business, war, philosophy, and psychology. Bernie followed Dave into the office, his big tail brushing against the oak furniture.

Dave sat down, picked up a pen and his Post-it notes, and scribbled, "Sell your business." He tapped his pen. He tried not to think that he may have cancer. Whatever it was, he'd find a way to beat it. He was always in control. He'd find a way to win.

Bernie nudged his cold, wet nose against Dave's elbow. Dave patted the large dog. "You know anything about selling a company, big guy?" The dog grinned, happy for any attention.

Kathy yelled from upstairs, "Dave, can you come up here?"

Dave chuckled. Control? The one person he had a hard time controlling was Kathy. Then again, he always liked a challenge. He had to figure out his business, and he didn't want to be bothered, but he put the pen down and climbed the stairs, locking the stairway gate behind him so Bernie wouldn't follow.

"Honey?"

"I'm coming," he said.

He went to the bedroom.

Kathy was standing in front of a tall mirror. She held up two long dresses, one red and one purple. Both dresses still had the tags on them. Either one could have cost several hundred dollars. "Which one do you like best?"

"The red one."

"You didn't even look."

"Ok. Purple."

"Dave."

"What?"

"I want to look good for dinner this weekend."

"Dinner?"

"We're going out with the Bragowski's, remember?"

Dave clenched his jaw. He was already meeting Mark tomorrow afternoon. He forgot that Kathy and Melissa had made dinner reservations. "When did you get those?"

"Today."

Dave thought he heard a cash register bell. Controlling himself, he tried to deflect. "Which one do you like?"

"I don't know."

"Well, go with the red."

Kathy's lips pursed. "We're going to "Jim's on the Bend." I think I'll go purple."

Dave rolled his eyes. He started toward the stairs.

Kathy tossed the red dress on the bed. "Wait. I want to talk about Italy."

"I would love to, but I have other things on my mind. Could we discuss this tomorrow?"

"Are you worried about your shoulder?"

"The doc didn't seem too worried, but I don't like that he sent me to a specialist."

"Sounds like just a precaution," Kathy said.

"I hope so."

"He said it was probably nothing, right? Let's just go with that. Think positively. And if it's something we'll have to deal with, we'll deal with it when the time comes."

Dave shifted. "All the same, maybe Mark's right. Maybe it is time to look into selling."

Kathy said, "Of course it is. You've worked hard. You've built a great company. I'm sure you'll cash in. Think of all the trips we'll take."

"I've got a lot to do, though."

"Dave, you're a pro. You always win. You've got this, honey."

Dave appreciated her kind confidence. Though she liked to spend the money he made before he made it, her encouragement made it easier for him to catch up. "Yeah, I've got some work to figure out. Plus I'm a little tired."

"You can do it. Just imagine. In a few months we'll be relaxing in Italy."

"Thanks." He hugged Kathy. She leaned into him while holding the purple dress up to her neck. "If you don't mind, I have some research to do. It may be a long night. I'm meeting with Mark tomorrow, and I want to make sure I know what I'm talking about."

Kathy lowered the dress. "If Mark can do it, I'm sure you can do it better."

Dave kissed Kathy on her head. He laughed at the red dress lying on the bed. Glancing at the price tag, he remembered the news about Don moving to Connecticut. He paused.

"Is there something else?" Kathy said.

"What?"

"You looked like you were about to tell me something."

Dave shuffled his feet. "You're going to find out anyway. Don and I talked today. He got an offer with Goldman Sachs."

"Really. That's great!"

"Yeah, except he's going to have to work in New York. He's taking the family to Connecticut?"

Kathy's face dropped. "Oh."

Dave nodded. "I hate to miss the grandkids," he said.

"He doesn't want to buy the business?"

"I asked him. Sounds like his mind's made up."

Kathy sat on the bed, still holding the purple dress. The red dress lay flat on the bed next to her. She paused, staring at the wall.

"I'm sorry, honey."

"Well, when you sell, we'll just have to make a lot of trips."

"Yes."

"You know I can't go long without seeing my grandbabies."

"I know."

Kathy put her hand in a fist and hit the bed. "Damn!"

Dave wanted to change the subject. "You know, for Saturday night, you should go with the purple."

Kathy stood again, holding the purple up to her neck. "I don't know. Maybe red is better."

Dave chuckled. "I have work to do." He left the room, leaving his wife to contemplate her dress dilemma.

A CLOSER LOOK

The news of a business sale affects several parties, especially those in the immediate family. Not only will the business owner have to manage his own emotions, driven by the pressures from his circumstances, but he'll also have to manage the dreams, hopes, and desires of his spouse and children.

If the business stays within the family, as in an inside buyer, then the family members, including the business owner, make their plans with the expectation that they will maintain some influence over the business after the sale. This comforts some family members because there remains a semblance of control over their future income, even if it is only an illusion.

When the business owner sells outside the family, either to a third party or even to his employees, the business owner soon realizes he will be separated from the business, ending his daily demands while bringing about a significant change in lifestyle for himself and his immediate family.

The family members will react in any number of ways. Some will develop fear because they believe the business to be a security blanket. After all, it provides cash flow for the family for years. The prospect of that change creates uncertainty. Thinking of themselves, they may not consider that the business may be facing market challenges, that it's not running optimized, or that a sale, if done properly, could drastically improve the family's financial situation.

A sale also creates questions about future income. How will the family source the necessary cash flow needed to live? Will they acquire it from the stock market, insurance products, interest rates, or alternative investments? The immediate family may not know these things, and the complexity of a financial plan can cause anxiety.

Another reaction, however, is the opposite of the above and is represented by Dave's wife, Kathy. The idea of a sale implies they've made it. They've struck gold! Won the lottery!

But wait. Nothing is earned until the documents are signed, the ink is dried, and the cash is in the bank. Her imagination, though, doesn't care. She can't help but imagine a higher income, a better life, and financial success. She has confidence in her husband. He's fought all these years to find income and pay for exciting vacations, a big house, a college education, his expensive trucks, her little Mercedes convertible, and Bernie the Saint Bernard. She believes the amount of money will be enormous, and they'll never have to worry about finances for the rest of their lives.

What Kathy doesn't know is what Dave is just now discovering. The sale of a business sounds great, but it's more complicated than it seems.

The spouse's reaction will have to be managed along with the sale of the business. Her extreme emotions of fear or excitement may influence the business owner's emotions, causing vulnerability in the sales process. This could hurt her dreams as much as his. In this case, what they both don't know can hurt them.

DECISION

Dave opened the gate at the bottom of the stairs. Bernie wagged his large tail, brushing it against the wall. Dave sat in his office chair and leaned back. Was selling the right thing? Was he jumping the gun? The doctor's news shook him. He had to admit it. But was he overreacting? What was best for Kathy? For him?

He scanned the pile of papers. Momoney's custodial statements sat on the stack he had pushed aside earlier. He picked them up. Underneath it was a letter from Frank

Addington, his CPA. He chuckled. Which mattered more: his accountant or his financial advisor? He put down the papers.

His Post-it note said, "Sell your business." He scribbled "Bragowski" underneath it. Then he wrote, "Don's out." Who would he sell to? His daughter, Katelyn? He thought about his employees. Shouldn't they have a chance at ownership in the company?

There were so many questions, and he needed information. No matter. He was in control. He could find the information and make it work. He had always found a way. This time would be no different.

9
DAY 2 THURSDAY
8:15 A.M.

The following morning, rain fell as Dave pulled into Fine-Line Manufacturing. Before he left home, he loaded his golf clubs into the back seat, hoping the rain would finish by the afternoon. He needed time to think, and the driving range was his favorite place for relaxing and putting his thoughts together.

He felt different this morning. For years, Dave began his days showing up to work and thinking of success and growth. This time, however, he was thinking of selling. What was that supposed to feel like? It seemed counterintuitive. If he sold a product to a customer, he would work to make sure he delivered. But this time, if he sold his business, he'd be gone. Would it be as simple as handing over the keys? He entered the front office door, his hand on the handle, his eyes focused on the door lock. One day that lock would belong to someone else. But not unless there's a buyer, he thought.

He stepped into the reception area. Ava waved hello as she transferred calls. Dave liked how Ava was answering the phone. Buyers would like seeing that, he thought. He strutted down the hall. He passed the pictures of office parties, the employees working hard in the warehouse, and the trade awards FineLine Manufacturing won from industry trade associations. His office personnel worked on their tasks. Things were quiet, but he felt good, like a man about to sell his business and win the lottery. He had earned it. He had worked hard all these years. It was time to cash in. He felt like a million bucks; he'd sell for several million. Manifest destiny with hard work, and he'd win again.

It was all within his control.

He landed in his office seat. Papers covered his desk. No matter, he was ready to begin his research. He pushed the papers aside and turned on his desktop. While it booted up, he scanned his inbox tray. Sales letters. Junk mail. He threw them in the trash bin. Soon, he wouldn't have to worry about any of those.

Diane knocked on his door.

"Hey," Dave said.

She held a paper in her hand. "There's a problem."

"With what?"

"CWB. They want to go out to bid."

"We have a contract."

"Don't shoot the messenger."

"Did they give a reason?"

"No."

Dave leaned back. "Hold on a second." He picked up the phone. "Tim, would you and Cliff come to my office?"

Diane put the paper on his desk as Dave hung up the phone.

"Is this how they notified us?" Dave said.

"Yes."

"Who sends faxes anymore?"

Diane shrugged.

Tim and Cliff appeared in Dave's doorway. Dave motioned for them to come in. "Shut the door." The door clicked as Tim pressed it shut. The two men stood next to Diane, waiting.

"Diane, tell us what you know."

"CWB sent a fax informing us they are putting a bid out for our gears."

"With a fax?" Tim said.

"Yes." Diane said, "They didn't give a reason."

"Don't we have a contract with them?" Tim said.

Dave said, "We do, but like any contract it has conditions for termination. Now tell me, did we get that order out on time yesterday?"

Tim said, "We made sure it got on the delivery truck."

"Cliff?"

"Yes, sir. They're our largest customer. My SOP is to track the CWB shipments each morning."

"There were no issues?"

"No, sir. In fact, I called Larry in their warehouse this morning. I do that every few weeks or so, but since we had the issue yesterday, I wanted to make sure everything was alright. He gave me no indication anything was wrong."

"You didn't tell him about the shipment coming unwrapped yesterday, did you?"

"No, sir."

"Were there any problems with the gears?"

"All passed quality control," Tim said.

"Have we given them any reason to break the contract?"

Tim and Cliff glanced at each other.

"What?" Dave said.

"Well, we heard from Larry that MarkDown Gears has called on them."

"MarkDown. They sell junk!"

Tim shrugged.

"So you're telling me we've upheld our end of the contract. There's nothing we've done to give them cause to break the contract."

"We've upheld our end of the contract."

"They must be looking for a lower price." Dave rubbed his forehead.

"Could we sue?" Tim said.

"Last thing I want is to get in a lawsuit with our largest customer. Especially not now."

"Why not now?"

Dave caught himself. Shoot. He was about to give away his thoughts of selling. He had to think of something quick. "Is there ever a good time?" he said.

"Good point."

A CLOSER LOOK

Inside the business owner's mind, the idea of selling grows larger and larger. In reality, however, the business operations must continue. He does not stop being a business owner just because he's thinking of the future. Customers still must be served. Employees still must be managed. And the cash must still flow. The difference, though, is it has stopped being business as usual for the business owner. Another risk has appeared, one that is far more personal than before. If the business experiences any setback, even the appearance of one, it could mean a loss of significant value during the sale. It could also severely impact his retirement standard of living. If he is unprepared, this new reality may fluster the business owner, compounding his risk.

The sooner a business owner recognizes this internal pressure, he'll be better equipped to handle the external pressures of managing his business. He must keep juggling the balls in the air without dropping any. This is hard enough when selling looms in the distance and it distracts him from managing his business. It gets more difficult when the prospect of selling gets closer.

DECISION

Dave sent Diane, Tim, and Cliff out of the office and had them shut the door behind them. He picked up the phone and dialed CWB.

The echoes of a busy warehouse came through Dave's receiver. "Marge here."

Dave said, "Hi, Marge. This is Dave Garrity at FineLine Manufacturing."

"Hi, Dave."

"Hi. We just received a fax from you that you're putting a bid out for gears."

"That's right. Are you going to bid?"

"Well, that's why I'm calling. We already have a contract with you."

"But that's for the three-quarters. We need one for the three-fifths."

Dave looked at the fax. "I'm sorry, Marge. I'm not seeing anywhere here that specifies the width."

"Hold on." The sound switched from the busy warehouse to the recorded CWB sales pitch for callers on hold.

Dave controlled his breathing as he waited, half-listening to the CWB story, but studying the fax to make sure he had the correct information. After a few moments, the warehouse sounds returned.

"You know what. We did not specify the dimensions in that fax, did we?"

"I'm looking at it, and I'm not seeing it. I just want to make sure we've done everything we can to take care of you."

"So far, so good. We've had no problems. In fact, Larry tells me your guys called him this morning to check on him."

"Thanks. I'm glad to hear that. So we're still good?"

"Yes. We'll send out a new bid request for the three-fifths. You're welcome to bid."

"We'll send one over as soon as we get the specs."

Dave hung up the phone and leaned forward. Crisis averted . . . or was it? Companies don't make mistakes like that, and now all his competitors have just seen a bid request from his largest customer.

He picked up the phone. "Hey, Diane. Be on the lookout for another bid request from CWB. They wanted a specific gear but forgot to mention it in the request. They're going to correct the specs and resend."

He hung up the phone, opened his drawer, and slid the CWB fax into a file he named "Legal."

10
DAY 2 THURSDAY
12:55 P.M.

Dave and Tim returned from lunch. The morning rain had moved on, and the sun shined through low-hanging clouds. The sun's rays highlighted a soft mist that drifted above the black asphalt. Inside Dave's truck, his golf clubs clanked as he rolled onto the parking lot. He might get some shots at the driving range after all.

He and Tim had discussed options for the new CWB bid, deciding whether or not they should adjust the terms of their current contract by adding a price addendum with the inclusion of orders for three-fifths gears. Normally, Dave would force the contract "as is" while making an entirely new one for additional products. With selling in the back of Dave's mind, however, he was more agreeable to altering the terms of the existing contract for the new product with an addendum.

Dave had other thoughts, though; uncomfortable ones. As he entered FineLine Manufacturing, he wondered if the purpose of the three-fifths bid was a replacement for the three-quarters that he was already providing. Did Marge lie to him? On top of all this, the last thing he wanted was to give anyone the impression he was thinking of selling. If his customers found out he'd be up the creek.

Ava said into the phone, "Yes, he just walked in," she gave Dave a look that said he'd want to take the call.

As Tim continued down the hall, Dave stopped next to his receptionist. "Who is it?" Dave mouthed.

Ava shrugged and spoke into the microphone, "May I tell him who's calling?"

Dave expected the caller to be Bragowski's secretary confirming their three o'clock appointment. "Is it Terri?"

Ava shook her head. "I'll transfer you to his office." She pressed a button.

"Who is it?" Dave said.

"Some man from Conqueror Capital," she said.

Dave cocked his head. That wasn't Mark's secretary. "Thanks." He went down the hall to his office.

Diane jumped up as Dave approached, holding some papers. "Dave, I have an issue."

"What is it?"

"We've not received the new CWB bid yet."

"Did they issue any statement notifying of a mistake?"

"No."

"We'll give them until tomorrow. Let's not worry until we have something to worry about."

Diane nodded, sat down, and returned to her computer.

Dave shut the door behind him as he walked into his office. He appreciated how much Diane cared about her work, defending his company. He was proud to have employees like her. People like her should have a chance at company ownership. Maybe selling to his employees would be the best for everyone. He'd get this guy off the phone, do some quick research on selling his business to his employees, and prepare for his meeting with Bragowski.

He picked up the phone. "Dave here."

"Hi, Dave. This is Bill Steele. I'm a regional president with Conqueror Capital. We're a private equity company that specializes in manufacturing acquisitions. You may not have heard of us, but we produce several goods across the globe. As I was looking across the landscape, I came across FineLine Manufacturing, and I was wondering if you might be interested in selling your business."

Dave blinked, and a shiver ran down his spine. The timing was too coincidental. He had to think quickly. How did Bill find out? Did he hear it from someone? Did Bragowski tell him? Did Kathy? Did Don? Does anybody else know?

Was this the same firm that approached Bragowski's company, or was it purely a chance call?

Dave held his breath. He had to play it cool. Maybe he could get some information out of this guy. The truth was, he had never had a call like this. Could he handle it? Was he prepared?

Of course! He was Dave. He was in control! He had run a successful cash-generating business for decades. He had fought at the negotiating table, selling his ideas to large customers, and winning every day. He could do this.

"Are you interested in buying?" Dave said.

"We're always buying," Bill said, "for the right opportunity."

Dave used his best poker voice. "What makes you think this is an opportunity?"

"We do our research."

Dave liked the sound of that. "What did you find?"

"Reasons to explore further."

Dave shifted in his seat. An image of him and Kathy walking through the Italian countryside popped into his mind. Heck, forget a two-month vacation; they might buy a villa over there!

Dave composed himself. "Do you mind if I ask what reasons?"

"It's a combination of things, Dave. We like to buy subsidiaries for our primary industries, taking advantage of market weaknesses using segmentation."

"What weaknesses are you seeing?"

"Dave, I appreciate your asking, but that's proprietary. And none of this matters if you're not looking to sell."

Dave closed his eyes, thinking. This guy was sharp. And if Bill Steele hung up the phone, he might miss a huge opportunity. As the questions ran through Dave's mind, he struggled to decide how to answer. A bead of sweat formed on his forehead. Dave was losing control of the conversation - and quickly!

"Well, Dave. Are you?"

Dave bit his tongue. He had to regain control, but how? If he said he wasn't looking to sell, this call would end and Conqueror Capital may run to buy one of his competitors. God forbid they acquired MarkDown Gears. Kathy would never forgive him for missing an opportunity like this. Heck, in her mind, she believed he had already made the sale. And if private equity capital flowed to a competitor, he'd have to fight harder to maintain market share, which would affect his valuation, let alone the sale of his business.

He had to face the fact that he didn't know enough yet. What should he do? Sell to his employees or sell to a third party? It would be one or the other because doing nothing was not an option. He knew his business had value, he just didn't know how much. If only Don wanted to buy the family business. That would have simplified things. Still, no matter. He was in control. There was no way he would let three decades of effort, time, and money just slip away...or would he?

How should he answer? If he said he was interested in selling and word got out, that could create a series of issues. How would he handle them? Could he do his research in time?

Then an idea popped into his head. Maybe he could keep Bill hooked long enough to get more research and formulate a plan. String the guy along. Then, when other buyers arrived, he'd choose the highest bidder. Could he manage his own deal?

Was it possible Bill Steele with Conqueror Capital was the first potential buyer? Would others come along? He had to believe so. He should plan accordingly. Yes, sir. Italy was in his and Kathy's near future. He couldn't wait to tell her. As she reminded him last night, he's got this.

"Anything can be bought, but for the right price," Dave said.

"Great," Bill said. "We're up in New York, but we'd like to come and meet you next week. Are you and your wife available for dinner?"

"When were you thinking?"

"How about next week?"

"I can arrange that," Dave said.

"Perfect. We'll send you an evite."

Dave hung up the phone. A few minutes later, an email popped up in his inbox. It was from Bill Steele at Conqueror Capital, requesting a dinner meeting next Wednesday. He stared at it while questions ran through his mind.

A CLOSER LOOK

As business owners hope to control the situation, their naivety at the experience of selling a company often leads to mistakes. One common mistake is giving hints about selling before they have decided to sell. Even asking about how businesses sell can trigger the hounds of potential buyers. The only problem with that is those buyers sense an opportunity - and one that is not favorable to the business owner.

In just a few days, several people had witnessed Dave's sudden curiosity about selling: his wife Kathy, his son Don, Mark Bragowski, and Melissa Bragowski. What Dave didn't realize was how fast word could spread. Any of them could have leaked it. But was it also possible this was just a chance call? Was Bill from Conqueror Capital any indication that other buyers were interested in his industry?

He remembered that Ava had answered the initial call, and Dave shuddered thinking how potential buyers were calling through his staff. What if Ava got wind that he was selling? She could spread the word to the rest of his employees. That would cause all sorts of problems, problems that could ultimately devalue his business.

Whether he liked it or not, Dave's world has changed. He had been running his business a certain way for several years, building a lifestyle expectation for his family and employees. But now things could change quickly – and that could either be very good or very bad.

A circumstantial phone call is rare. It's likely not a coincidence when it occurs near the time when the business owner considers selling. That means someone in his circle knows. When word spreads outside the business owner's primary network, he's lost control of the secret, and in the competitive game of business, he who knows has the upper hand. The business owner had better be ready for a challenge he had not expected.

DECISION

"I thought it was going to be a short call," Diane said.

Dave stood at the side of Diane's desk. "Sorry. Took longer than I thought."

"Everything alright?"

Dave paused. "Yeah. Why wouldn't it be?"

Diane frowned. She held a piece of paper.

Dave took it. "New CWB bid?"

"Yes."

"Requesting three-fifths?"

Diane nodded.

Dave took a deep breath. "Okay. I'll get Tim and we'll work out a deal."

"Let me know how I can help," Diane said.

Dave had handled calls like this before, but today, with the added pressure of selling his company, he worried about his reputation. Bill Steele's call was on his mind. If selling was his goal, this was not the time to lose a customer.

He went into the office and shut the door. Dave wiped another bead of sweat off his forehead. Questions swirled in his mind. His meeting with Bragowski was coming up, but he didn't want to wait. He needed information. He called Tim. "Did you see the bid?"

"Yes, sir. Three-fifths gears."

"Work out an answer based on what we discussed. I have some appointments this afternoon. Tomorrow morning, let's fine-tune the new proposal and send it off to them. I'll want them to have our bid by eleven at the latest."

"Will do."

Dave hung up the phone. He left his office, told Diane he would be out the rest of the day, said goodbye to Ava, exited the front doors, and climbed into his truck. If he was going to sell his business, he had to take some action and do it now.

11
DAY 2 THURSDAY
2:05 P.M.

Dave stood in the bookstore row. The odor of paper drifted between the aisles while elevator music hummed softly from the overhead speakers. He picked the book off the shelf. The title read, Profit, Paradise, and Piña Coladas: The Ultimate Guide to Selling Your Business and Living the Dream. The cover showed a man and his wife on beach chairs and enjoying a beautiful Caribbean sunset while sipping their cocktails with tiny umbrellas. In the distance, a dolphin jumped next to the silhouette of a sailboat. He thought the cover and title were a little much. But the idea did feel good. He didn't need an island, after all. He'd be content with an income in retirement that afforded him and Kathy a few more vacations, a beach house, and his new big truck to show off at the senior breakfast meetings and the country club parking lot.

He flipped open the cover and scanned the "Table of Contents."

Chapter 1: "Diving into Dollars: Selling Your Business Without Getting Soaked."

Dave laughed. He could appreciate the humor about such a serious subject. At least the author first organized his thoughts about money. He flipped to the chapter. Paragraphs and charts adorned the pages, including bubbles with palm trees. Do they have palm trees in Italy? Dave wondered.

Dave picked three more titles off the shelf: Gold Bars and Golf Carts: The Lavish Life After Selling Your Business, Sell Like a Sultan: Transforming Your Business Sale into a Royal Affair, and Sell Your Business Like a Shark: How to Beat Them at Their Own Game and Buy a Private Jet.

"These should get me started," Dave said. He flipped through the pages of the "Sultan" book. The first chapter was titled: "Diamonds in the Sand: Investing Your Windfall with Flair." Dave liked the sound of that. He would outdo Bragowski's flair.

"Hello, Dave."

Dave twisted, hiding his books near his chest. It was Dr. Cal White, his dentist. The man stood a few feet away.

"Sorry. Didn't mean to startle you," Dr. White said.

"Hey, Cal." Dave quickly put on his sales face while sliding the books behind his back. "Good to see you."

Cal grinned. Being a good dentist, he always found a way to show off his smile. "See anything good?" he asked, pointing at the rows of business books.

Had he seen what I was holding, Dave wondered. Does Dr. White know that I'm thinking of selling my business? Best to play it cool. "No. Just seeing what's out there."

Cal said, "I always buy too many books. Never enough time to read them all, though. The ones that keep my attention are those that tell a story and intersperse it with facts."

"I hear you," Dave said.

"See you at next week's breakfast meeting."

"Will do," Dave said. As Dr. White walked away, Dave held his breath. He scanned the room. Did Dr. White figure out what Dave was doing? Did anybody else see him with a stack of "How to Sell Your Business" books? Dave had to hurry, buy the books, and hide them in a bag before anybody else noticed.

Seeing no other potential witnesses, Dave tucked the books in a bundle under his arm and fretted if Dr. White figured out what books Dave was buying.

A CLOSER LOOK

While there are many books about "how to sell your business," most of them make two major (and faulty) assumptions. First, they assume the business is sellable. Second, they assume the business owner can sell the business by himself.

What Dave won't learn from these books is that the numbers are against him. Of all the businesses that open, only 20% of those are ever listed on the market when it comes time to sell. But listing is only that - listing. Unbeknownst to Dave, of those 20% listed on the market, only 20% of those ever sell. Twenty percent of twenty percent. That means just 4% of all businesses will ever sell.

If that's not bad enough, it gets worse. Of those 4% that sell, surveys state that more than 50% of business owners who do manage to sell experience some form of regret. This regret can come in many forms: feeling pressured to sell either by the market or life circumstances, unsure of what he'll do with the rest of his life, realizing he could have sold for more if he had only been better prepared, or any other numerous reasons.

Thus, only 2% of all business owners achieve a happy ending. That means 98% do not. Those are low odds.

Preying on this concern, many How to Sell Your Business books play into the business owner's desire for control. After all, it's what he's done with his business for years. If he can control his business, he can control the sale of his business. At least that's what he's thinking.

What's more, trying to capture control of the situation can also make him realize how little control he has. This can lead to paranoia if he's not careful. Has he mistakenly revealed that he is thinking of selling? Has someone observed his behaviors and deduced what he intends to do? Will people whisper about his behavior? Have his employees discovered his intent? Have his customers? What will he do if anyone even suspects he is thinking of selling?

These questions and others run through his mind. Finding himself in a new environment, Dave, like most other business owners, welcomes any message that will give him more control. It can come from research, conversations, advice, seminars, and books. Facing the challenge of a business sale is a process he's never done. Thus, his ears will naturally gravitate to pleasing suggestions that will minimize the risk. He is only human, after all. But the enticement of success can blind him to the risk-laden trap he may never see coming.

DECISION

Dave walked to the cashier. He laid his four books on the counter.

"Will that be all, Sir?" the clerk asked.

"It's about all I can read in one day," Dave said.

The clerk smiled as she put the books in a bag. "Pulling an all-nighter?"

"Yeah," Dave said. He thanked the clerk, grabbed the bag of books, and headed to the door.

"Next, please," the clerk said as the door shut behind Dave. Dave strutted to his truck, the wind in his hair, and the sun in his face.

"I've got this," he said. "Things are going to turn out well."

12
DAY 2 THURSDAY
2:15 P.M.

Dave threw his books in the passenger seat and shut the door. His golf bag lay in the back seat. He put his hands on the steering wheel. He looked at his watch. "Thirty minutes," he said. He didn't want to arrive at Bragowski's business too early. He'd appear too eager if he did. But he didn't want to drive around either, and he was too nervous to be caught in the parking lot reading. "Thanks a lot, Dr. White," he said to himself sarcastically.

He had to do something. Move anything forward. Anything. He had twenty-nine minutes. What could he do?

He had to think. So much had happened in the last two days. Just yesterday morning he thought he had everything made. His business was running. Kathy was happy. His bills were paid. He had all the right toys.

Now, he had a health question. His wife was pushing him to keep up with Bragowski. His son wasn't going to buy his business. He received a strange inquiry from Conqueror Capital, and he wondered if the whole world knew he was considering selling. What should he do? He still liked the idea of selling to his employees. "What was that called again?" he asked.

With the engine running, Dave opened the center console. He pulled out his reading glasses, and put them on. He opened his web browser on his smartphone. "Okay. Who would handle employee ownership options when an owner sells?" He typed "business owner sells to employees" and pressed "enter". Immediately, the Employee Stock Ownership Plan (ESOP) appeared on the screen.

"ESOP. I've heard of that."

Dave scrolled through the information. The letters were small. There was so much information. As he adjusted his glasses, he felt old. Tired. He had to admit the last few days wore him out. He wasn't as young as he used to be. Selling was probably the right way to go. But if he would sell to his employees, he would go out the hero. Do the right thing. Do the admirable thing and take care of his people. An ESOP sounded like the right choice. He read the advantages: "Continuity, Simple and Easy, Tax Advantages, Employees like it, Flexibility."

"This may be the answer," he said to himself. "Go the ESOP route first, and if that doesn't work string along Conqueror Capital as a backup." He liked having options. In his mind, his options were growing. He could do this, he thought. Do like he'd always done. Outwork everyone. He'd keep going. Gain momentum. He was in control. He imagined that trip to Italy. Maybe he'd buy more souvenirs than Bragowski, and Kathy could show herself off with all the bags of Italian clothes she'd buy.

He scrolled some more. Then he saw the disadvantages of ESOPs: "Costly, Time Consuming, Regulations, Employee Allocation Risk."

"How much would it cost? How much time? And what regulations?" Dave said. He had to hurry and sell if he was going to plan that trip. He didn't want disadvantages to get in his way. But the last thing he wanted was to deal with regulators while selling his business. He would need the advice of an expert. Did his CPA, Frank Addington, understand ESOPs? He had never mentioned an ESOP in their twenty-year relationship. And what about hiring a lawyer? He wanted to bypass spending money on advisors. By relying on his own abilities he saved his money and avoided unnecessary expenses. Though it was taxing and tiring, his customers loved him because of it.

All the same, he had a financial advisor, Richard Momoney. Dave had just seen statements from him the previous night. Every quarter, Momoney deducted fees from his account, and those went to pay Richard and his firm whether the stock market went up or down. What was Dave paying him for each month? He was already paying him for advice, and Richard's information about selling his company would surely be covered by the fees he was already paying. "Time to earn your money, Richard," Dave said. He typed a text. Assigning Richard to a research mission about ESOPs might justify this quarter's fees so long as the information was worthwhile. Dave hit "send", and his text flew off into cyberspace.

Dave set the phone down and leaned back in his chair. He looked at his watch. Five minutes. He had just enough time to get to Bragowski's. He put his truck in gear and drove onto the main road, imagining that, in a few months, he and Kathy would be looking out their villa window at the Italian countryside.

A CLOSER LOOK

Many well-meaning business owners are appreciative of their employees. Thus, when his family member opts out of becoming a buyer, the next natural thought is to give the employees first right to buy. After all, they helped build the business under his leadership. Would they not appreciate being repaid with ownership in the business?

An Employee Stock Ownership Plan (ESOP) is a not-so-common method to achieve the sale of a business to its employees. Many owners explore this idea first because it makes them feel good. They research the process. They learn quickly, however, that there's more to ESOPs than originally imagined. ESOPs can be complicated vehicles where the stars must align, requiring several players to help execute the transaction. What Dave doesn't yet know is that the transaction may not make sense for his financial goals, the employees', or both.

Not knowing what he doesn't know, Dave proceeds anyway and explores the ESOP option. He does this by inquiring with other professionals: his CPA, a business attorney, or his financial advisor. Which one he calls first will be up to him.

Before the transaction is completed, however, he'll have to talk with all of them. In doing so, Dave discusses with others that he is considering a sale, which in and of itself can create new challenges he may not see coming.

DECISION

Two months until Italy. Funny, yesterday morning, he only thought of his doctor's appointment. Now, he imagined a successful business sale whereby he and Kathy would one-up the Bragowskis both in his retirement account and on their two-month trip to Italy.

He had to press on if he was going to catch up, though. Dave drove through the streets, plotting his meeting with Mark Bragowski in his mind. What questions would he ask? What would he reveal? Should he mention anything about Conqueror Capital? Did Mark explore an ESOP? He steered his truck into Bragowski's parking lot, and he pulled up alongside Mark's big truck. He was not going to be intimidated. He imagined a successful meeting, just like all the sales calls he ever made. "I'm in control," he said. Bragowski may have sold first, but Dave was confident he would sell best.

13
DAY 2 THURSDAY
3:00 P.M.

Dave sat in the waiting room. Terri offered him a cup of coffee, but he declined. His leg bounced while he sat. It was just like Mark to make him wait. He looked at his watch. It was ten past three. Mark's booming voice echoed through his closed office door and down the hall. The man was on the phone telling the story of his latest outing. How did he keep so quiet about selling? Or did he? What exactly was his strategy?

Mark's door opened, and his voice came through the doorway. "Send him in!"

Dave stood before Terri could answer. "I heard him."

She nodded. Dave walked into Mark's office. Golf tournament trophies adorned the shelves while pictures of Mark's hunting and fishing successes hung on the walls. A photo frame of Melissa's and Mark's kids sat on his desk. Unlike Dave's Post-it-covered desk at FineLine Manufacturing, Mark's desk was spotless. There were no loose papers or Post-it notes; just his laptop and a notebook.

"Dave, how's your day going?" Mark stood and gave him a hearty handshake.

"Good," Dave said. "Your desk is clean."

"Yeah, I figured it's time. You sleeping alright? You look a little pale."

Dave blinked. Was it becoming obvious? "I'm good." He did not want to mention the doctor's appointment. No telling who Mark would tell. Or did Kathy already tell Melissa? He hadn't thought of that. He had to change the subject, and Mark loved the attention. "Congratulations again on selling. That was big news."

"Thanks. I'm surprised myself how the whole thing came about." Mark sat back in his chair and pointed across the desk. "Have a seat."

Dave took the chair, and his height suddenly shortened compared to Mark Bragowski. For a brief moment, he felt like George Bailey when he sat across from Mr. Potter in "It's a Wonderful Life".

Mark leaned forward and put his elbows on his clean desk, like a man who had just cleaned up the competition and prepared to share his ultimate business wisdom with all lesser beings.

Before Bragowski could gloat, Dave leaned in. "So, tell me about it."

"Not too much to say. One day the phone rang. It was a firm out of New York. They flew down here, took Melissa and me out to dinner. Later we shook hands on a tentative deal, something they called an IOI. An "Indication of Interest.""

"Who was the firm?"

"Can't say yet. Not until the deal's done."

"You're not going to tell me the terms, either, I suppose."

"Let's just say it's more than good. It's very good."

"Had you been looking to sell?"

"Not really. But as you and I both know everything's got its price."

"I'm just curious, but why didn't you decide to sell to your employees?"

"When someone comes at you with a briefcase full of cash, you talk with him."

Dave leaned back in his chair. He wanted to know more, but would Mark even tell him? Could he tell him? "Kathy says you and Melissa are going to Italy."

"Yeah. It's a small reward for all we're getting out of this deal. I figured it wouldn't do any harm."

"But what are you going to do when you get back?"

Mark's face stiffened. It was the first time since his announcement that his face lost its shine. "I'll think of something. Trips. Consulting, if I feel like it. Lots more hunting and fishing. And I'm sure you and I will be getting a lot more rounds of golf in."

Dave wasn't getting anywhere. He would get more information reading his Sultan and Shark How to Sell Your Business books than continuing this meeting. He decided to do what he always did with Mark: get right to the point, but in a way that irritated Mark's ego. "It sounds like you won the lottery. Completely random. Congrats, again."

"Now hold on. I wouldn't say it was completely random."

Dave's tactic worked, as it always did. He raised his eyebrows and said, "Oh?"

"I've run a good operation here. My business has provided cash flow for decades. When your seeds have grown into trees that bear fruit, someone is bound to want to harvest it."

"So you're saying just wait until someone comes calling?"

"Why? Are you looking to sell?"

"Not really," Dave lied. It was the second time he'd done that, and it still bothered him. "I'm just curious how the process works."

"I'll bet Kathy likes the idea of you selling."

Dave shuddered but then caught himself. "Yeah."

"Tell you what. When this deal comes through, I'll send my buyers your way. They do this sort of thing all the time. If I put in a good word for you, who knows. Maybe you and Kathy can join us in Italy."

Dave didn't want to tell him that Kathy already suggested that. "So what business advice would you give now that you're in the process of selling?"

Mark pointed at a large picture on his wall, one taken after a deep sea fishing expedition. Mark stood proud next to a large swordfish that hung next to him. "Captain your ship right, and you'll bring home the prize."

"Thanks," Dave said. He stood, smiled, and shook hands with Mark. He left, said goodbye to Terri, and exited the building. "Captain my own ship. Stay in control," Dave said. "Exactly what I've been doing for years. Except why does it feel like I'm taking on water?"

A CLOSER LOOK

When looking for information, it's natural to ask those who have either sold their business or are in the process of doing so to share their experiences. While it's attractive to go this route initially, a business seller can only relate to his own experience. His business is unique. It has specific qualities. It offers specific products and specific services. It serves a niche. Its competitors have developing demands. The detailed experience of one business seller can be vastly different from the experience of another. This means that information taken from one business seller's experience may or may not apply to the business selling strategy of another business owner. How will the current business seller know whether or not to include all or parts or any of the advice he receives from another business seller?

Unfortunately, business sellers who have completed a transaction will also likely share their experience in a positive light, even though the statistics mentioned above state that only fifty percent are satisfied after a sale. Why would an unsatisfied business seller share their experience in a positive light? It's called "saving face". Ego and reputation have a lot to do with it, and seeking information from sellers runs the risk of having that information twisted to suit the seller, not the information seeker.

As Dave learned, seeking information from the one going through a business sale adds another layer of complexity. The seller may not want to or be allowed to share the details of the transaction because those details are either still developing or because both parties don't want any interference from third parties while they are in negotiation. They can't give you specific advice about selling pertaining to your business, and they are hampered if they try. The reason for this is non-disclosure agreements, also known as NDAs. When parties are in negotiations, there's often a signature required by both parties promising that neither party will reveal proprietary information to a third party or use information gained for undue benefit. This adds confidence and accountability that discussions with each other can proceed in good faith. Revealing proprietary information to a third party, including disclosing information about products, processes, and personnel, gives one party a legal repercussion over the other. The end result is a challenge in acquiring strategic selling information from a business owner who is currently going through the business selling process.

Thus business sellers - the successful, the unsuccessful, and the ones still going through the process - are not the best and most efficient source of information.

DECISION

Though Dave had looked forward to his meeting with Mark, he now felt more confused. If Mark's success was completely random, what conditions existed to allow for that opportunity? There was always something to be done. If you went fishing, cast the line in the right place, reeled the bait in the right way, and pulled at the right time, you caught your fish. Was selling a business any different?

Mark Bragowski made it sound like he got the sale just because he was Mark Bragowski. Kathy often fell for Mark's bravado through Melissa, and she pushed Dave because of it. But Dave never operated that way. He'd make his own luck. If he would sell, he'd make a plan and figure it out.

First, he needed to decide which path to take.

14
DAY 2 THURSDAY
4:00 P.M.

Dave pulled into the golf course parking lot, unloaded his golf clubs, and walked toward the driving range. Within minutes, he had a bucket of balls and teed up his first golf ball. He held his driver, retreated the club, and swung his hips. He brought the club down low. He hit the ball with the inside of his club. "Slice!" he said as the ball whipped from left to right. "Gosh darnit!"

He teed up a second ball when suddenly his cell phone rang. He told himself he'd ignore it but, then again, it might be important. It was the same thing he always told himself. He looked at the phone. When he saw the name, he snatched it up. "Richard!"

"Hey Dave," Richard Momoney said on the other line. "Got your message about ESOPs. Do you have a minute?"

"You bet. I was worried you were playing golf or something."

"Not today. Tomorrow maybe. You want to join me?"

"It depends on what you tell me," Dave said.

"Ok. Here's the scoop. ESOPs have pros and cons. First, the pros. Employees tend to like the sound of them. Though none of them understand what they are or how they work, it can motivate them to work harder both before the sale completes and after. There may be tax benefits for the seller, but you'll have to talk with your CPA about that. And the employees have more say about the direction of the company since their retirement is tied up in the value of the business."

"Okay," Dave said. "But what about me?"

"Well, that's where we have to talk about the cons."

"Great."

"First, for the employees, having their retirement in the value of one company can cause some issues for them, mainly a high concentration of risk, lack of diversification, and illiquidity. It's because of this that some employees may be wary of the deal. And as for you, their lack of understanding about the business's valuation, as well as the complexity involved in just administering the thing, could railroad the situation. And oh yeah, last I remember, you once told me you had a bit of debt on your books. An ESOP tends to work better when the company has very little debt, and that doesn't include too many companies out there."

"So, I just have to manage the process and it will all work out?"

"It's not that simple, Dave. The fact is the situation for an ESOP has to be perfect. The stars have to align. If your business or the politics of the situation vary too much, it could be a disaster."

"Is it worth looking into further?"

"I'm never one to forgo doing more research," Richard said, "but because it's a business sale, you need to be careful about what spreads through the grapevine. Be sure to seek confidentiality as you go through this process, and only deal with people you can trust."

"Uh, huh."

"I wish the ESOP process weren't so complicated," Richard said. "If there were an easier way, I'm sure more people would do it."

Dave had an idea. "How about you? Would you know anybody looking to buy a business?"

"I am licensed," Richard said, "But the regulators wouldn't want me near your business sale with a ten-foot pole. So introducing you to a buyer is out of the question. I do know people in our brokerage house who can help with ESOPs, but whenever I send someone to them, it seems ninety percent of the initial calls don't get a second. I don't want to discourage you, but I've gotten to the point where I don't want to give people a false hope. I just want you to know it's not as simple as it sounds."

"So you think I should avoid it?"

"I'm not saying that," Richard said. "Again, more information can be a good thing, at least to help you decide. It's just been my experience there may be better ways to proceed. All the same, do you want me to pass your information along to my brokerage house?"

Dave thought of his call with Bill Steele and Conqueror Capital. His mind shifted to negotiating with them. If the process with them was more favorable, he'd go that route. "No thanks. Not right now, anyway."

"I do have another thought," Richard said.

"What's that?"

"I know a business broker, but actually he prefers to go by the title 'M&A Advisor'. Bob Miagi. Good guy. He deals with this sort of thing all the time."

"What's his fee? I bet it's pretty high."

"I don't know, but it's up to you if you want his help. If you want to talk with him I can make the introduction."

Dave's books sat in his truck. He had a lot of reading before him. He still didn't like the thought of shelling out money when he could learn how to sell his business himself. Also, he felt uncomfortable letting another person know he was thinking of selling. He could handle it, but it was turning out to be a lot to handle. "Not yet," Dave said.

"Okay. Either way, when the cash is in your hands, I can help you invest it," Richard said.

"Understood." Dave said. He thanked Richard for the information and hung up the phone.

A CLOSER LOOK

While Employee Stock Ownership Plans have a place in the business seller's options, there's a narrow window of conditions in which they make the most sense - especially for the business seller.

The biggest issue, though, is an unnamed one. The business owner is the center of the business. The employees work for him. When he leaves, the center of the business also leaves, leaving a giant hole inside the business. While everything looks good in theory, a business transitioning from a central leader to a democracy among employees will face near-term and potentially long-term instability.

Whether or not the business owner sells to a third party or his employees, he must establish his business processes in order for all the parties - banks included - to agree to participate. Yes, the business owner may be confident in how he runs his business, and his employees may be great people, but their enthusiasm can blind them to the reality that the business must be able to operate independently from the business owner. If this is not established prior to the sale, the sale can damage everyone. And if the sale doesn't happen, the business owner is left holding the bag.

DECISION

Dave swung his golf club and hit ball after ball. For every good shot, he hit five bad ones. It wasn't his day. He had too much on his mind. He could not concentrate. He had one more ball left.

His phone rang again. He looked at the caller ID. It read "Dr. Blackwood Skin Care." His shoulders slumped as he picked up the phone. "Hello."

"Mr. Garrity. This is Dr. Blackwood's office. You're scheduled to come in next week, but we have an opening tomorrow morning. Would you like to reschedule for 8 a.m.?"

Dave sighed. "Might as well get it over with."

"Thank you, Mr. Garrity. We have you on the schedule tomorrow morning at 8 a.m. We'll see you then."

"Thank you." Dave hung up the phone. He had one more ball. He teed it up, bent back, watched his back, and kept his arms straight. He then gritted his teeth and swung his arms with all he had.

The club hit the ball but hooked wide left into the net, falling far short of his target.

15
DAY 3 FRIDAY
8:35 A.M.

Doctor Blackwood leaned into Dave's shoulder, his light shining on the spot. "Is it cancer?" Dave said.

"Not sure. Doesn't look like melanoma. But it has an irregular shape."

Dave sat still, letting the doctor do his investigation. The cold air chilled him. He felt embarrassed, his shirt off, his belly expanding over his waist. After his debacle at the gym and his lower energy, he decided he would return to the gym. Maybe he would hire that trainer.

Then again–.

"We're going to take a sample. This may pinch a little."

The doctor held up a long metal object. It looked cold and surgical. Dave didn't like the looks of it.

"Okay. Just a little."

Dave held his breath. He felt a prick, more than a little. "Ouch!"

"Got it." Blackwood handed the steel tool and the sample to his assistant. She put the sample in a small dish and left the room.

"How serious do you think it is?" Dave said. His shoulder stung.

Blackwood pressed his lips together before he spoke. "Just looking at it, it appears to be a cross between a cherry angioma and a basal cell carcinoma."

"Are they malignant?"

"One is. One isn't."

"So we don't know."

"I wish I could be more clear. Visibly it could go either way. But a lab test will give us a definite answer."

"How long until the test results?"

"We tell patients about two weeks, but that depends on the lab's workload. If they're busy it could take a little longer. As soon as the results come in we'll let you know."

"Okay." Dave stared at the floor. "Maybe I spent too much time at the beach."

"Maybe."

"I have a beach condo. Mainly use it for clients, but sometimes my wife and I just like to get away."

Dr. Blackwood didn't answer as he wrote on his notes on his clipboard.

The assistant returned.

Blackwood said, "She'll bandage your shoulder. We'll send the sample to the lab. Once we hear from them, we'll call you right away. I'll be available after if you have any questions."

"What options would I have in a worst case scenario?"

"There are a lot of scenarios. But in your case, the odds are there's a treatment for it."

"Thank you," he said.

"If it is anything, better we get on top of it now. You did the right thing by getting it checked. We wouldn't want anything too aggressive to get out of control."

Dave nodded. Blackwood and his assistant left the room, leaving Dave alone to put on his shirt. He tried not to wonder if his life was being cut short. He liked to think of himself as twenty-five years old. Thirty, even. But that was over half his life ago. How many more years did he have left? How many more doctor visits?

He left the room. Walking down the hall, he passed two more people, both advanced seniors. Their hair was white. One was in a wheelchair. The other walked with a walker. He said hello to them both as he left the waiting room.

He exited the building. "Seniors," he said. "Hell, I'm a senior, too."

A CLOSER LOOK

Doctor visits increase with age. It's a common trend, but it's one we don't like to think about. Yet in the typical business sale, retirement isn't the only consideration. Health is, too. Doctor visits can increase due to a number of factors.

First, there are generally increased health issues. These can range from chronic conditions, such as hypertension, heart disease, diabetes, and arthritis. These often require regular monitoring and treatments. Also, these increased health issues can occur simultaneously, requiring more frequent medical attention to treat and manage multiple medical conditions at once.

Second, preventive care and screenings increase. Regular screenings look for cancer (mainly breast, colorectal, and prostate), osteoporosis, and eye disease. The aim of preventive care is early detection and treatment which often require follow-up visits. Sometimes, vaccinations are recommended as a treatment, and these can increase the need for additional visits.

Third, medication management requires the experience of a medical professional, especially in the case of polypharmacy where a patient takes multiple medications at once. These visits are necessary to reduce the risk of side effects and dangerous drug interactions by evaluating dosages and the safety of medications.

Fourth, with the increase in age, there is a greater risk of injuries due to falling. This comes from factors like loss of balance, reduced vision, and muscle weakness. Post-fall doctor visits are common, along with future visits for preventive care. Bone health is a serious concern, as fractures can cause not only falls but additional problems for the life of the patient.

Fifth, many experience mental and cognitive decline as they age, including dementia and Alzheimer's disease. Regular medical visits help monitor these conditions.

Sixth, natural age-related changes, such as hearing and vision loss, require frequent visits. Nutritional monitoring and lifestyle adjustments may be necessary to maintain metabolism, physical activity, and quality of life.

Finally, physical therapy visits, while maintaining the health of the individual, take time away from work and can put pressure on the business owner and his business.

One must think of health-related expenditures and downtimes as they look to sell their business. And, if married, both the husband and wife will age, leading to a greater chance of medical expenses for one, if not both, members of the couple. An unsuccessful business sale, whereby the transaction price and profit do not meet the business seller's retirement needs, will significantly increase the medical costs as a percentage of "cost of living." Medical expenditures will eat into the hopes and dreams of his retirement.

DECISION

Dave called Kathy from his car. She picked up immediately. "How'd it go?"

"We don't know yet."

"What?" Her voice rose in shock.

"Waiting for the lab results."

"How long?"

"A couple of weeks."

"They didn't give you any indication?"

"No. The doc seemed confident if there was a bad diagnosis that it could be treated. He said it was good I came in early."

"I wish I had pushed you there when I first noticed it."

"That's okay. I'm here now."

"Whatever it is, you can handle it. You're a winner."

"I'm in control."

"Absolutely! I'll see you when you get home."

"Will do," Dave said.

"Love you."

"Love you, too." Dave hung up the phone. He had to hurry back to help Tim with the CWB bid. With the questions surrounding his shoulder, and now his largest customer putting out bids while he was researching selling his business, Dave felt more out of control than he had in years.

16
DAY 4 SATURDAY
7:00 P.M.

The neon sign overhead flashed "Jim's on the Bend." Dave stepped back as the valet drove his large truck from the restaurant entrance around the corner.

"Look at him," Kathy said. "You'd think he's watching Don go off to college again."

"What?" Dave spun around.

"Oh, don't be so hard on him," Mark said. "A great truck is like a great horse. You feel uneasy until they hand the reins back to you."

"You're right," Dave said. "A truck that big and you worry if someone is able to handle it properly."

Mark slapped Dave's shoulder. "It'll be alright, big guy."

The hostess opened the door. "Welcome," she said.

A waiter took the dinner jackets off Kathy's and Melissa's shoulders and hung them in the attendant's closet. "You'll have to excuse Mark," Melissa said. "Ever since New York came calling, Mark's been talking about horses."

"Horses?" Dave said.

"Thoroughbreds," Mark said. "Racehorses. I've got my eye on a foal right now."

"What do you know about thoroughbreds?" Dave said.

"They're damn expensive, for one! And not just buyin' 'em. The upkeep over the years can be dozens of times that! And you never stop at just one!" Mark and Melissa laughed heartily as the hostess led the foursome to their table. Kathy gave Dave the look. She expected her ship to come in just behind the Bragowski's, and better.

Better than racehorses!

Dave shook his head. The four sat down at their booth. While the attendant poured their water, Mark said, "I'm taking the little lady with me up to Lexington next week. The mare's expected to drop her foal and we want to be there."

"Where is this place?" Kathy said.

"Diamond Dynasty Ranch," Melissa said. She brought out her phone and showed Kathy pictures of majestic green fields, solid barns with golden hinges, and fence posts with diamonds carved out of their post caps.

"Dave, let's go with them!" Kathy said. "I want to see this place."

Dave remembered his calendar. When was his meeting with Conqueror Capital and Bill Steele? Wednesday? Should he mention it tonight? Should he deflect? Kathy was putting him on the spot again. He didn't want to appear unsupportive of Mark Bragowski. He might need his advice and experience in the future, but he also didn't want to show his hand too soon. If word got out that he was selling, how would he manage his employees?

"You know, I imagined tonight we were going to talk about Italy. I didn't expect anything about racehorses," Dave said.

Melissa leaned into Mark. "We've had all sorts of ideas. It's been fun to talk about all the things we plan to do."

Mark Bragowski nodded, but there was a slight twinge in his forehead. A wrinkle. A sign of worry, perhaps? If Dave hadn't known Mark for so long, he might have missed or overlooked it. But despite Mark's attempts to hide it, Dave sensed a bit of unease. Mark lifted his arm and squeezed Melissa toward him. "Darn right. Once you've struck oil, the world opens up to you."

Kathy, not to be outdone, leaned into her husband. "I've been telling Dave it's time to sell, too."

"See. I told you Kathy would like you to sell," Mark said, slapping his large hand on the table.

"Okay. I admit I've thought about it," Dave said.

"More than that," Kathy said. "I'm planning our trip to Italy. We intend to go along with you."

"That would be wonderful!" Melissa said.

"Next thing you know she'll want to buy a racehorse." Dave said.

Kathy's eyes flashed. "And why not?"

"See, what'd I tell you."

"You know, what if you did come up to see this foal," Mark said. "Why don't we go into thoroughbreds together?"

"What a great idea!" Kathy said.

"I don't know the first thing about racehorses," Dave said.

"Neither do we," Melissa said, "but Mark just does what he always does. He dives in and finds a way."

Kathy squeezed Dave's arm. "Oh, honey. Let's do it!"

Dave was losing control of the conversation. If this were a negotiation, he'd be losing. It was tough enough to hide the fact that he was considering selling while learning the process. To make matters worse, his friends and family acted like the money was guaranteed. But was it really? He wouldn't mind the racehorse idea, except it was premature. He was disappointed in Kathy. Didn't she already have a nice car and a beach condo in Destin? She was entranced with the Bragowski's selling and all the opportunities that could come with it. But Dave was not Mark Bragowski. He had to figure out what was right for himself and his own family. He did not know his company's valuation. He did not know what Conqueror Capital was going to offer.

"Excuse me," Dave said. "I'm going to run to the restroom. I'll be right back."

"We'll be here," Mark said. "Now, ladies. What shall we name our horse?"

Dave hated to leave but, in his negotiating training, he knew that sometimes leaving the table and returning after a few minutes often equaled out negotiations. It was the only way he could regain some control over this conversation and, temporarily, his life.

A CLOSER LOOK

The idea of selling a business is exciting. Who wouldn't want to imagine the potential windfall and opportunities for a new life in retirement? Like any other investment, however, the danger lies in the extremes. Most business owners, approximately 97%, don't know their true transferable business value. When a business owner imagines potential hobby expenses, such as travel or toys, he can get sucked into dreaming of an extreme sale price before he even has an action plan.

To make things worse, the hopes and dreams of people who depend on him, such as a spouse and children, add pressure to the business seller. This pressure can make the business seller lose sight of his selling execution and instead leave him focused exclusively on the rewards. It's the classic advice: "Don't count your chickens before they're hatched." Yet it's so easy to do exactly that.

The business owner must become aware of his emotions regarding his selling strategy and his retirement dreams. While dreaming can be okay, he cannot let it overtake his thoughts on his selling strategy. Early in the selling process, when he begins taking those first few steps, his strategy and his dreams pull him in different directions. If he imagines an impractical business valuation (as do 75% of all business owners), it's easy for his retirement dreams to exceed reality. Unrealistic retirement dreams only put pressure on his family, his employees, and himself. He'll risk adding to his vulnerability if his retirement dreams are not in line with the situation.

Dreaming is fun, but it must come with the right plan.

DECISION

The valet returned Dave's truck. He quickly scanned the sides to make sure there were no new scratches.

"See. She's in one piece," Mark said.

Kathy and Melissa laughed. Dave tipped the valet, said goodbye to the Bragowskis, and opened the door for Kathy to climb into his truck.

When they drove home, Dave didn't know what to say.

Kathy said. "I'm so excited. Imagine that. Actually own a racehorse! What if we win the Kentucky Derby?"

"Why not the Triple Crown?"

Kathy rolled her eyes at Dave's sarcasm. "What will we name him? How about Mystic Breeze, or Royal Tempest? Oh, there are so many options."

Dave rubbed the back of his head. "You're getting a little ahead of yourself, aren't you?"

Kathy's tone changed. "You know, anything Mark can do you can do better."

"Sure I can."

"If Mark can sell his business, you can sell yours for more."

Dave remembered the hint of worry on Mark's forehead. It was there only half a second, but it was there. "He hasn't sold anything yet."

Kathy leaned back and crossed her arms. Kathy was never one to like having her dreams challenged. The two of them sat, their mouths closed, while Dave drove the truck home and the rock songs they remembered from the 70s and 80s played on the radio.

17
DAY 6 MONDAY
8:15 A.M.

After a tense Sunday, Dave looked forward to getting back to work. He never liked it when he and Kathy weren't speaking, but after the drive home Saturday night, it was obvious that something had come between them. Dave wanted what she wanted: security, nice trips, experiences, toys. Thankfully he was able to save on taxes over the years by declaring his car and his beach condo as a business expense. That contributed to more of his personal income. But selling? This was all new to him. He liked having a plan, and things seemed to be happening so quickly. On the one hand, he wanted to hope for a favorable outcome. On the other, how could he be sure the outcome would be favorable if he didn't know what he was doing?

Dave passed Ava as she spoke into her headset. He turned the corner just as Diane ran toward him. "We have a problem."

"I just got here."

"You're not going to want to wait. CWB sent a notice canceling our contract."

"What!" Dave pressed her into his office. The other employees watched, concern on their faces. Dave shut the door. "They can't do that!"

"Here's the notice."

Dave snatched the paper from Diane's hands. The subject line read: "Termination of Contract Effective Immediately." He skimmed the remainder of the fax. "They don't give a reason."

"What do we do?"

Dave pulled the CWB contract from the "Legal" file. "Says here there's a sixty-day notice. I was surprised myself when they agreed to it, but it's in there, and they signed it."

"Should we call our lawyers?"

Dave sat in his chair. He picked up the phone. "I'm calling CWB." He dialed the number, keeping the phone on speaker so Diane could hear. After several rings, a voice said, "Marge, here."

"Hi, Marge. Dave over at FineLine Manufacturing."

"Hello, Dave. What can I help you with?"

"Well, we just got a fax from you saying that you're canceling our contract."

"You did? Hold on."

Dave waited while the echoes of CWB warehouse noises came through the speaker. In the distance, Marge's voice said, "Hey Larry. Did you send that fax to FineLine?"

Larry's voice was muffled.

"Can you make it out?" Dave whispered to Diane.

Diane shook her head and mouthed, "No."

Dave tapped his pen on his desk and bit his lip.

"Dave," Marge said, her voice now loud over the speaker.

"Yes."

"I'm sorry about that. We meant to send that to someone else."

Dave leaned forward. "So you're not canceling our contract?"

"No, sir. That was for another vendor."

"You know, you may not want to do that again. You're bound to give someone a heart attack." Dave smiled, trying to be humorous.

"I apologize," Marge said.

"Could you send us a follow up fax documenting the error?"

"Sure, Dave. We can do that."

"That would be great. Thanks."

"You have a good day."

"You, too." The phone line went dead. Dave hung up. "What is going on over there?"

Diane shrugged.

Dave picked up the phone. "Tim, can you come to my office? We need to discuss CWB." Dave hung up. "He's coming back here."

"The CWB account is twenty-five percent of our business. What will we do if we–."

Dave lifted his hand. "I'm not going to hear it."

"But we should plan–."

"One thing at a time. Let's just first make sure the account is secure.

A CLOSER LOOK

A common mistake business owners make is achieving unbalanced success, meaning the business owner acquires a large customer or two that makes up a huge percentage of his business, and then he believes his business is valuable for a prospective buyer. But this is a shortsighted way to look at things. While it can make a business, one large customer can also break it. Market forces are always at play. Thus, a business owner whose business receives a disproportionate amount of its income from a single source may not realize how fragile his business situation is. It's called Concentration Risk, and it's very real.

A business with a large customer needs to learn from serving the customer how to acquire other same-sized customers in the same way. Diversification spreads Concentration Risk. Without that diversification, the business remains vulnerable to market forces and swinging cash flows.

To make things worse, a business seller with Concentration Risk may become blind to his risk exposure because of the cash flow his family receives. He imagines a prospective buyer will appreciate his "solid" business cash flow. What he doesn't understand is the prospective buyer will likely devalue his business due to Concentration Risk and lack of revenue diversification.

Thus, the business seller is caught in the middle. He wants to pretend he's made it while, at the same time, he hasn't. He then becomes vulnerable to additional selling emotions, which can leave him at a disadvantage against the buyers at the closing table. This is usually a preventable problem before getting to the closing table.

DECISION

Dave told Tim to shut the door behind him. "Something's up with CWB."

"What is it?"

Diane gave Tim the paper. "They sent an erroneous fax canceling our contract."

"They did?"

"We called and talked with Marge. She admitted it was for another vendor."

"Not us?"

"No, thank God. She said she was going to send another fax clarifying the error."

"You think they will?"

"They'd better. After last week's mishap, something is wrong over there."

"I'll say," Diane said.

"I don't know what it is, but we need to be on top of things. I want to make sure every order is double checked for quality before it goes out. Put your best of the crew on each shipment. Run through the checklists. And call their guys. Strengthen those relationships. Let's write down everything to make sure we solidify our position."

"Yes, sir." Tim marched out of Dave's office.

Diane stood before him.

"What do you think?" Dave said.

"I'll feel better when we get their correction."

"Me, too."

"You think it will come?"

"I'm going to say yes. But, just in case, I'd better call our contract lawyer."

"Do you need my help?"

"Just keep an eye out for that fax."

"Will do." Diane left the office. Dave stood, went to the door, and closed it. He returned to his desk and picked up the phone, except he didn't dial his lawyer. Instead, he called his accountant. He kept his voice down so it wouldn't travel through the door. "Hi, Frank. Dave Garrity. Yeah, I know it's been a while. Hey, I want to know if I can come in to see you tomorrow. I need to talk with you about selling my business."

18
DAY 7 TUESDAY
10:15 A.M.

Stacks of files and papers covered the desk. Dave leaned to one side so he could see his accountant, Frank Addington. Frank was a short man, balding with a mustache. A pair of wire-rimmed glasses sat on the crest of his button nose. His shoulders seemed small in his business suit and his loosely knotted tie around his neck. Frank's fingers punched some numbers on the keyboard.

"So, I'm considering selling," Dave said. "I figured it would be smart to talk with you before I do."

Frank typed more on his keyboard. Then he reached over to his calculator and, without looking at it, hit several numbers with his fingers. Then he returned his hand to the keyboard, never taking his eyes off the computer screen. "Mmmm, hmmm."

Dave leaned around the stack of files. "Well, what do you think?"

Frank typed some more. "Well, let's see. Last I checked, you have good owner's comp."

"Exactly, that means–."

"But you have some tight percentages with operating expenditures. Your EBITDA is stable. . . for now."

"What do you mean by that?"

Frank typed some more. Dave wondered if he heard the question.

"I see your expenditures are a little high. Did you ever reduce your shipping and production costs like we discussed last time?"

Dave cringed, thinking about the wrapping that failed around last week's CWB shipment. "Yeah. We did."

"How much?"

"Negligible."

Frank set his glasses higher on his nose. "Mmmm, hmmm."

"So, if I'm going to sell, I need to come up with a valuation."

Frank typed some more on his keyboard. "Yeah, we'll talk about that."

"What else should we talk about?"

"Your ratios."

"My ratios?"

"Yes." Frank typed some more. Then he reached down to his calculator again, typed more numbers with his fingers, and returned his hand to his computer.

Did the man even see the last numbers he calculated? "What are you talking about?" Dave said.

Frank stopped typing. He shifted in his seat and pushed the stacks of files and papers to the edges of his desk. "Dave, I hate to tell you this, but your business isn't ready to sell."

Dave leaned back, blinking. "What do you mean it's not ready?"

"Now don't shoot the messenger. I'm just giving you some insight."

"Go on."

"As I said, you're paying yourself a good amount, but several of your ratios are off, and your growth the past few years has been muted. Now, I'm no expert on your industry, but I have several clients actively selling and I'm hearing from them how important the "growth story" is to buyers." Frank lifted his fingers and made air quotes as he spoke.

"I'm the owner. Shouldn't I also get the highest paycheck?"

"It's not just the paycheck. It's also the balance sheet. Here. Look at this." Frank twisted his computer monitor so Dave could see it. "It's your owner's equity. Cash may be coming in, but it's also going out."

"That's what happens in a business."

"True, but at varying degrees. You want much higher incoming cash than outgoing cash. That adds to investment, new products, markets. You know, that sort of thing."

"Well, of course I want higher incoming cash. That's how I can pay my salary."

"I understand. But if your goal is to sell your business, you're stretched thin."

"A new owner would like the cash flow I make."

"Well, they might. But it depends at what risk."

"You financial guys. All you talk about is risk."

"That's our job."

"Well, it's mine, too. That's how I build my life."

"That's good. But you're paying me so you can keep it."

Dave sat back. "So what should I do? Pay myself less and reinvest it back into the business?"

Frank folded his hands together. "Dave, I'm not a business consultant. I'm only telling you what the numbers say. While your business pays you today, a prospective buyer may not value it as high as you would."

"What would you value it, then?"

"A common rule of thumb is to consider a range of three to five times earnings. Because your cash flow is what it is, you're looking at a range of $2,400,000 to maybe $4,000,000 at best."

"What?!?!"

"Again, don't shoot the messenger."

Dave clutched his chair's armrests. "You can't be serious."

"I'm only giving you the numbers. And remember, it's not what you make, it's what you take that matters. In other words, for many types of businesses like FineLine, it's not top-line gross revenue that buyers are interested in, it's net income. Basically, what's left over for shareholders after expenses have been paid."

"This is ridiculous. I've worked at this for 30 years, put my own money in it to get it started, employed hundreds of people over the years, fended off lawsuits, built a nice lifestyle for me and my family, survived 4 recessions, and you're saying that all that is only worth $4,000,000??"

"A business buyer isn't just paying for his own salary and some profit along the way. He also wants a future return on investment, and these days he's probably looking for a huge growth story." Frank twisted his fingers in his folded hands. "I'm sorry if this news disappoints you."

Dave stood. "No. Thank you. Will you email me your analysis? I need to think on this some more."

Frank typed on the keyboard. "They're in the portal. You'll get an invite in your email inbox shortly."

Dave shook Frank's hand and left the building, rubbing the back of his head on the way to his truck.

A CLOSER LOOK

When taking the idea of selling to an accountant, more often than not the accountant's advice will be that it's not time to sell. There are two reasons for this, however. The first may be that the business is, in fact, not in a position to sell, including many of the reasons mentioned earlier in this book. A good accountant will understand financial documents and point out any areas of concern that a buyer would notice. These numbers remain subjective, but they can be helpful in preparing a business seller with his strategy.

The second, though, may not be so obvious. The advice against selling may come from the accountant's concern with losing an important client. While a business pays the owner and the employees, the business also pays accountants, and more than what individual clients pay them. This means that a business client is quite valuable to a financial professional regarding his own cash flow, and the accountant would have an incentive to keep it. If the business owner sells, the accountant would likely lose a valuable client and a significant portion of his own cash flow. Thus, if the business has any problems in relation to a business sale, the accountant would be incentivized to caution the business owner against selling rather than offer a strategy to prepare the business for a sale.

Fortunately, the majority of accountants are professionals. But they are also human. The business owner would be wise to do his due diligence on his own numbers. This helps verify that the accountant accurately expresses logical concerns if he advises the business seller not to sell.

While it's important to talk with your accountant, it's also important to evaluate the advice you receive. It may be true that your business is not ready to sell. It may also be true that your business could one day become ready to sell. There's a big difference, and that difference determines your strategy. Thus, when the advice is, "Not yet," it's either a delay designed to help or a delay designed to stall. It's a question of motive. The business owner will have to determine which it is. If your accountant doesn't give guidance to help build a strategy toward your goals, you'll want to evaluate his participation with your team.

When the accountant does give the, "You're not ready yet," advice, the next question is how will the business seller take it? Probably for the first time, his dreams of wealth are being challenged. His business has value, but there's a 75% chance it's not nearly as high as he imagines it to be. What does that do to his ego? Will he handle it well, or will he not? With all the pressure building, this moment will become critical. This is when the business owner will make his choice. Will he do things with his own friends or network, or will he seek the right help and be willing to pay for it?

DECISION

Dave shook in the driver's seat of his truck. He had half a mind to fire Frank Addington right then and there. $4,000,000! What was that guy smoking? Who was he to tell him his ratios were off and that the growth story of FineLine wasn't strong enough? Dave paid himself what he should pay himself, and he was doing the best he could to grow. He would not feel guilty about buying his truck, taking Kathy on their vacations, or owning a beach condo in Destin.

Except now he was selling. He was still trying to figure everything out. It had only been a week since he got the news from the doctor, and with Mark selling, that only added to the pressure. What if Frank was right? Frank had helped him get to where he could pay himself the cash to provide the lifestyle he and Kathy wanted. Was Frank telling the truth? What was his business worth? Only $4,000,000?! That couldn't be right. He had to drive back to the office and look at his numbers.

Only he couldn't. Not today. Not in his state of mind. If his employees found out he was looking at valuations, they'd know he was thinking of selling. That could derail the whole thing, especially his current paycheck and lifestyle.

It wasn't worth the risk.

Dave laughed. "Risk," he said. "That's all anybody is talking about these days."

Maybe it won't matter, he thought. Tomorrow he was meeting with Bill Steele and Conqueror Capital. He'd discover all he'd need to know at dinner tomorrow night. How many millions will they offer? Nine? Ten? While his mind skipped between thinking of seven and eight digits, Dave pressed the gas pedal and sped down the street.

19
DAY 8 WEDNESDAY
6:30 P.M.

The sun was setting in the west. Dave was back at "Jim's on the Bend." He stood alone at the curb as the valet drove his truck around the corner. Kathy wanted to come, but he advised against it. He had to handle this dinner with Bill Steele and Conqueror Capital on his own. It was, after all, their first meeting. No point in getting Kathy involved in the negotiations. She was too busy thinking of racehorse names, anyway, and one she came up with was "Conquering Conquerors." Dave admitted he did like that one.

Despite the pressure he was feeling - the news about the spot on his shoulder, the jealousy of Bragowski's selling, the expectations of running racehorses and trips to Italy, the CWB debacles, the hiding his interest in selling from his employees, and the ridiculous $4,000,000 valuation from his accountant - Dave reminded himself he would win. Kathy was right. He was the conqueror of conquerors. He was in control. He, not anyone else, dictated his company's value. And he would sell, accordingly. He'd ask for $15 million while offering to remain on board for a year to help with the transition. He'd be willing to walk away with twelve, but that would reduce his transition help by six months.

Bill Steele didn't know who he was up against!

A limousine pulled up to the valet, and the driver wearing a suit exited the limo and opened the rear door. A young man with dark hair and perfect white teeth stood tall and extended his hand. He seemed half Dave's age. "Dave Garrity?"

Dave nodded. "Yes."

"Bill Steele. Conqueror Capital."

The young man appeared polished. Probably Ivy League. Harvard Business School, maybe? Regardless, Dave felt confident knowing he had thirty years more experience than him. "Nice to meet you."

Dave didn't notice the limo driver opening the door on the other side. Bill said, "I'd like you to meet Max Hatchet. He's one of our numbers guys at Conqueror Capital."

Max Hatchet stood tall. A balding man in his sixties with a large Italian nose, his eyes bored into Dave like a vulture about to devour its carcass.

Dave shuddered. "You didn't mention you were bringing someone else?"

"He's our numbers guy. No doubt with the quality operation you run you've had talks like these before with other potential buyers. I figured you'd be expecting a numbers guy."

Dave blinked several times. No, he hadn't, but he wasn't about to admit it. He extended his hand to Max. "Nice to meet you."

Max said. "You, too."

Bill smiled with his sparkling teeth. "Shall we go in?"

The three were seated. As the waiter took their drink orders, Dave directed the conversation at them, hoping to build rapport. "I've got to tell you, Bill, you sounded much older on the phone."

"I've been with the firm since right out of school. I guess when you've done as many deals as I have, you get pretty good at it."

"I feel the same way about my business."

"What made you start the business?" Bill said.

Dave sipped his draft beer. "I was roughly your age when I was doing sales for an auto parts company. While I was there, I had an idea for a gear design no one else had thought of. I put together a patent, made a prototype, and offered a proposal to a medium-sized car manufacturer. They went with it, and I've been in business ever since."

"How's your market?"

"We focus on quality. So we're not the cheapest. Sometimes we have to remind customers of that when they try to move to a cheaper product. But then their gears break, and they come crawling back."

Max leaned forward. "If you don't mind my interrupting, could you forward the financials to me? I can look them over while you two are talking."

"Sure," Dave said. He picked up his phone and emailed the files.

Bill sipped his glass of merlot, the wine having no effect on the man's pearly white teeth. "Tell us about CWB."

"You know about CWB?"

"They mentioned your gears in some of their own marketing materials. I figured you were doing business with them."

Dave said, "You have done your research. I'm impressed."

"Lots of hours late at night will do that for you," Bill said.

"Well, CWB. We've had a good-sized contract with them for several years. Every so often we renew the contract, but the terms stay pretty much the same."

"Have they put out any bids lately?"

Dave raised an eyebrow. "Yes, but for a part we're not currently providing."

"Which one?"

"A three-fifths gear. We're currently supplying their three-quarters."

"Why would they want a different size?"

Good question, Dave thought. He was so protective of what he was providing, and thinking of selling, that he hadn't taken the time to ask why the new size. That brought up another thought. He suddenly realized he may have made a mistake in not having Conqueror Capital sign a non-disclosure agreement. What was he thinking? He bit his lip and forced his fear deep into his gut. He'll worry about that later. "They didn't say," Dave said. "We put a bid to them a few days ago, but they haven't announced the winner yet. Usually takes them a few weeks before they announce that we won again."

Bill raised his wine glass. "I like that."

Dave lifted his draft glass, clanking it against Bill's wine. "I'll drink to that." Dave, with his fear subsided, decided to trust Bill and Max across the table. Keep businesses about relationships, he thought. Handshakes. Those sorts of things. They could make an offer at any moment. Stay positive and in control. Things were going well.

"How many employees do you have?" Max said. His eyes remained glued to his phone, the soft glow reflecting on his imposing nose.

"Thirty-five, including myself."

"Any HR issues?"

"Very few. I'm fortunate to have loyal employees. When they come, they rarely leave. Some have been with me over fifteen years."

"CWB is your largest customer?"

"Yes."

"What percentage of your business are they?"

Dave hesitated. He didn't like where the questions were going. "Decent. Close to twenty-five percent."

"Who's your second largest?"

"That would be Aerolift."

"What percentage are they?"

"Roughly ten percent."

Max leaned over to Bill and whispered something in his ear. Bill nodded, keeping his grin going but his other facial features seemed less optimistic. "Dave," Bill said. "You said you were thinking of selling. What valuation were you expecting?"

Here goes, Dave thought. "$15 million."

Max and Bill didn't move, showing neither surprise nor disappointment. "How'd you come up with that?" Bill said.

"When you consider all the work that went into FineLine Manufacturing over the years, all the sweat and toil, all the effort it took by so many people to make the company the success it is today, I'd consider it's worth at least that." As Dave said it, he panicked at how naive and simplistic that sounded. Did he actually just say that out loud? Why hadn't he gotten at least a valuation estimate before this meeting? Or even years ago before even entertaining the sale? With so much of his net worth tied up in the company...50%?...60% or more??

Max leaned over and spoke with Bill again. Bill nodded, keeping his grin. "Dave, I hear you. There's no reason you shouldn't be proud of a business like that. That's why we reached out to you, and trust me when I say that we don't reach out to everybody. There's definitely potential in your business. But Max has been looking at your numbers. The multiples don't work at $10 million let alone fifteen. Quite honestly, he's seen many business financial statements in his forty-plus years of doing business. He tells me the documents don't explain your justification for that amount. The multiples are far less. That doesn't mean we're not open to hearing more, but you have to understand that I can't justify overpaying for a premium multiple to my partners at Conqueror Capital and the investors in our funds. To us, this opportunity looks more like $4 million. Maybe four and a half at best."

Dave did his best to keep his poker face, but this conversation had headed in a direction Kathy wouldn't want to hear.

A CLOSER LOOK

Dave is experiencing a common situation among first-time business sellers. His hopes and dreams, and his boundless sense of optimism, have helped him imagine an extreme business valuation, while the business buyer, one who has prepared for this scenario, has brought in the numbers guy to talk him down. It's a psychological game. The weakened position of the business seller stems from his own ego, his dreams, and his hopes. The buyers know that. What's more, they know the business seller knows that. The seller just has a hard time admitting it.

The business buyer's strategy has become highly strategic. By playing to ego, the buyer's tactic is to help the seller save face. Is he a smart business owner, or is he not? A business seller with an unrealistic valuation risks exposure as a fraud for not valuing his business like a professional. The buyer will shift to discussions about multiples, which can be confusing for a business seller since he isn't looking at or aware of his business's multiples on a frequent basis.

The business seller has a choice to make. Does he protect his business reputation by pretending he has business mergers and acquisition acumen, or does he set aside his ego and focus on the actual money he receives in a transaction? When selling a company, it's often not just the price that matters, it's also the terms that come into play.

What the buyer intends to do is play to the seller's ego, suggesting to him that he's smart enough to value a business "properly" as true private equity firms do, and take a "realistic" offer that any respectable business seller would jump at the chance to get.

Of course, the offer given by the buyer benefits the buyer, not the seller. The buyer's suggestion of a "proper" valuation remains subjective, even if it is based on financial statements and multiples. Unfortunately, the ego-vulnerable business seller is at risk of not knowing what the difference is if he falls into the trap set by the business buyer. And the whole time that the owner (now seller) has been running the company, he could have been building something that many buyers would be willing to pay a premium to own.

At the end of the day, the buyer hopes to prey on the seller's ego while drastically dropping the price, making a much lower offer, and having the seller thank them for giving him an offer well below his financial expectations.

It's a very clever strategy and it's one that happens every day.

DECISION

"Four and a half million?" Dave said.

"Likely four," Bill said.

"That's not what I was hoping for."

"You've seen Max's case. Any private equity firm in the country would value it for less, but we see the potential in FineLine Manufacturing. We're looking to partner with a business we can grow."

"What about my employees?"

"We've got a great reputation for helping them through transitions. Many of them become open to working with our subsidiaries, if that's how they desire to advance. And you'll stay on at least one year to assist in the meantime. It's a true win for everyone."

"Kathy won't like it."

"Don't be so sure. You'll still get your salary and benefits for a year while we transition. And, plus, your bank account will have $4 million of liquid assets. It's a reasonable situation."

Dave leaned back. "Of course, I won't get the whole $4 million. There will be other costs, like taxes and fees."

"Naturally."

"What do you say, Dave? Will you accept our preliminary offer?" Bill flashed his pearly white teeth. No amount of merlot could penetrate his smile.

Dave struggled not to appear defeated. Somehow he was glad he received any offer at all. "I'll have to talk with my accountant," Dave said.

Max's lips curved slightly upward. It was the first hint of a smile the man made all evening.

"Sure," Bill said. "Go talk with your accountant. We can write up the Letter of Intent and email it to you soon. That way there will be no question about our intentions."

"Okay. Well, I'd better get going." Dave said.

The three men left the table, walked outside, and said their goodbyes. After Bill and Max drove away in their limo, Dave waited under the street light for the valet to return his truck. Many questions ran through his head. Could he trust Conqueror Capital? Would Bill Steele and Max Hatchet undercut their offer more as they did their due diligence? What would the Letter of Intent contain? It all depended on the black and white, after all. And was Conqueror Capital his only chance? Could he find other buyers who might make a better offer?

Questions ran through his mind, many of which he found difficult to put into words. For the first time in his career, he had doubts about the business decisions that he had made over the years. Could he have hired better employees? Should he have fired some earlier? Were there other blocks of business he should have pursued? Were there new products he should have created? Were there customers in other geographies he should have gone after, or was he just too comfortable to go after them? He recognized a deep aching feeling in his gut like someone punched him in the stomach.

As his prized vehicle approached, Dave saw a scratch on his bumper. Did it just happen tonight? Was it always there? Dave wasn't in the mood to fight it. He just didn't know how he felt at all.

20
DAY 9 THURSDAY
8:05 A.M.

Dave was tired from the fight he and Kathy had last night. After he mentioned Bill Steele's offer to Kathy, she went through the roof. Even if he had wanted to sleep on it and think of a new plan, Kathy's emotions wouldn't have let him. Last night as he lay awake on his sofa, his phone had lit up. There was an email in his inbox from Bill Steele and Conqueror Capital. Attached was a Letter of Intent offer of $4 million.

Dave felt his blood boil. The insult caused him to roll back and forth on the sofa. He struggled to deal with his anger and hurt. He couldn't get it out of his mind that $4 million was all a private equity company thought his business was worth.

When morning had come, he didn't bother getting cleaned up. He had to get out of the house, and the first thing he thought of was to see Mark Bragowski. He rubbed his eyes. His hair was disheveled. His shirt collar was off in the back. He sat in Bragowski's waiting room. The morning sun rose through the trees outside the window.

Terri's face filled with surprise at Dave's appearance. "Was Mark expecting you?"

"No, but I really need his advice."

"He's in his office. He's got a big meeting today and asked not to be bothered."

Dave wiped a bead of sweat from his forehead. "It will only take a minute."

Terri picked up her phone. "Yes. . . Yes, I know, but Dave Garrity is here. . . I know. . . Yes, I'll tell him. . . He said it will only take a minute. . . Okay." She lowered the phone. "He is very busy, but you can go see him."

Dave stood. "Thank you." He walked past her and opened Mark's door.

Mark sat behind his desk, papers stacked all over. It was a far different desk than last time. Mark grinned, but something was different. Worry covered his face. "Hey, Dave. You okay?"

"Rough night."

"I'm sorry to hear that. What happened?"

Dave sat in the chair. "You're selling your business. I need some advice."

"I'm always glad to help a friend. You know what they say, what goes around comes around."

"Okay. I was approached by a firm out of New York that wanted to buy my business."

"You were? Congratulations!"

"I'm not so sure. I had a figure in mind, but they came at me with an offer that was less than half what I was looking for."

"Wow, less than half? That's not good. That's a bad place to start."

"I'll say. When I told Kathy about it, she just about blew up. I hadn't seen her that angry in years."

"That's why you look like you woke up on the wrong side of the bed."

"I'm just curious, did your buyers approach you with a valuation you expected?"

Mark leaned back and admired his fishing pictures. "They did. In fact, I'm on my way to the closing this afternoon."

"If you don't mind my asking, how did you come to the valuation you expected?"

"Simple. Elbow grease. When a guy works many hard years to build a company, that work has to pay off."

"I told these guys the same thing. It didn't go so well."

"Doesn't sound like they were the right buyers."

"I don't know. My accountant warned me that's about what FineLine was worth. I thought he was nuts. I guess he wasn't so far off."

"What do accountants know, really? Come on, Dave. We're the shooters, here. We take the risks. We get the accounts. We swing for the fences. That's what guys like us do. Don't get down if the first pitch is a strike. There'll be others coming."

"Kathy is upset, though. She sees your success and is envious."

"Well, not everyone can hit a home run their first time at bat. But that's okay. We're all in this game to win."

"What are you going to do tonight?"

"I'm not sure," Mark said. "Take Melissa out to celebrate. But more than likely after have a few drinks and sleep in tomorrow."

Dave stood. "I don't want to keep you. Good luck on your closing. I hope it goes well for you."

"You know, before you go, I came across something that may help."

"What's that?"

"Hold on. I got an email . . . " Mark searched on his computer with his mouse and keyboard. "There it is. Someone must have heard I was selling and sent me an email about some seminar. It's next Tuesday at the Grand Smoke Lounge in Buckhead."

"What kind of seminar?"

"How to sell your business. I don't know these guys, but it may be worth checking into. Here, I'll forward it to you. Why don't you register?"

"I hate seminars."

"Who doesn't? But you never know who you'll run into at those things."

"I guess you're right."

Mark stood, walked around the desk, and fixed the back of Dave's collar before he patted him on the shoulder. "It'll be alright, Dave. Give it a few days, and those guys may come at you with a higher number. Don't appear so eager. Maybe a little hard-to-get is all you need. And, who knows, maybe another buyer is right around the corner."

"That'd be nice to have some leverage."

"Leverage wins, my friend."

"Thanks," Dave said. He said goodbye and left Mark's room. He waved to Terri, exited the front doors, and climbed into his truck. He looked at himself in the rearview mirror. "Geez, I have bags under my eyes. I don't look well." He pulled a brush out of his glove compartment and combed his hair.

"What else do I need to do?" He had to regain his thoughts and control his situation. But it was becoming easier said than done.

A CLOSER LOOK

The initial reaction of a business seller after receiving a perceived low-ball offer from a buyer can vary from shock, sadness, and depression to outright anger. It doesn't feel good, especially when dreams of beaches and a comfortable retirement become less certain. This is the equivalent of a sports game, where you've prepared the entire week but the other team comes out, scores quickly, and never lets up. That wasn't the way it was supposed to go, yet here you are. What do you do? Do you stick with the current game plan? Or do you throw it in the trash and make things up as you go?

To make matters worse, reactions will also come from family and friends. A seller's spouse may have a completely different reaction than he does, preventing him from organizing his thoughts and processing his own reactions in his own way. This only adds to his stress and it prevents him from forming a new game plan.

Realizing he's vulnerable, the seller now goes to his closest confidants and asks for advice. He has to admit he doesn't know the answers, but he only wants to make that admission to people he feels safe with, and preferably those he won't have to pay.

Initially understanding that he's unprepared makes the business seller frightened. This fear is natural but very real.

And the fear expressed by his own family only multiplies his own. He has to get a grip on the situation, and quickly, for everybody's sake. But how?

Again, he'll seek advice from people he already knows. The only question is whether those people in this circle of advisors are the ones he needs now and in the future.

DECISION

Dave slammed his fists against his steering wheel. He was so mad at himself. $4 million. Was that all FineLine was worth? He had fought for years to be proud of his company. It just didn't make sense. As he pulled out of Bragowski's parking lot, he dialed Frank Addington and scheduled to meet with him that afternoon. He had to get to the bottom of his financial statements, and fast!

21
DAY 10 FRIDAY
3:30 P.M.

Frank Addington sat behind the stacks of files and papers, typing on his keyboard.

Dave leaned around a desk, trying to see the man as his fingers clicked the keys. "Frank," Dave said. "I have got to make these numbers work."

Frank stopped typing. "Work to do what?"

"To sell, dammit!"

"You told me they made an offer."

"Not one I'm willing to accept."

Frank shook his head. "If you'll recall, I suggested that several of your ratios are off. That and the lack of a growth story is why your valuation is what it is. That's why they made the offer they did. And keep in mind that that's just a starting point. Their next offer is likely to be far lower the more they dig into your business."

"But, you're my accountant. Aren't you supposed to arrange the numbers in my favor?"

Frank shifted in his seat, sat up, straightened his tie, and slid his wire-rimmed glasses above the crest of his nose. "Dave, I work numbers. I don't work miracles."

Dave stretched his collar around his neck. Was it getting hot in here? "Well, can you tell me why the ratios are off?"

Frank twisted his computer monitor. "Okay. Do you see this number right here? That's your operating margin. It's a relationship between your variable production costs and what revenue you have left. It's not a high enough number for your industry."

"Okay."

"That's got to improve. And see this number here? That's your ROA."

"ROA?"

"Return on Assets. It shows how well you're using your assets to generate a profit. A low number like this means your company isn't running as efficiently as it could."

"Is that all?"

"You see this number here? That's ROE, or Return on Equity. This means that the return to shareholders, meaning you, is lower than it needs to be and has been declining."

"Which means what?"

"Many of your trends are heading in the wrong direction. Any buyer is going to see that, Dave."

"Is there anything else?"

"Yes. You have too many toys."

"What do you mean?"

"Your truck, Kathy's car and your beach condo. You've been asking me all these years to include those on the tax returns as deductions. Remember, I've included some of it, though not as much as you wanted me to."

"I use those to get clients. . ."

Frank raised his eyebrows.

". . . in addition to personal use," Dave said.

"Buyers will wonder about your toys and perks you're running through the company," Frank said. "They're called 'add-backs' and they're generally frowned upon by most buyers, not to mention the lenders."

Dave rubbed the back of his neck. "Okay. So how do I fix it?"

"Improve the ratios. You can either take steps within your company to fix the top number by increasing your revenues, or you can go the other route and fix the bottom numbers by decreasing your costs, starting with those personal expenses."

"That would take time. Isn't there another way we can look at the numbers differently so that the ratios adjust?"

"We can remove your personal items from your business expenses but that would mean restating recent financial statements and amending tax returns."

"But won't that increase my current and future taxable income?"

"Correct."

"Kathy won't like that. Is there anything else we can do with the statements?"

"That depends. Have you withheld information from me?"

Dave leaned back in his chair. "Diane gives you everything, doesn't she?"

"She's the one who emails me, yes," Frank said.

"You haven't told her I'm asking you this?"

"No, sir. Everything you've told me is confidential."

Dave had to think. What was he to do? Would he go to Diane and risk exposing that he's considering selling? Should he just ask her if she's giving Frank all the numbers? Was there a chance that she wasn't? No, Diane was too good, too loyal. There would be no missing data. She would have given everything to Frank. What else could he do? He couldn't tell her to send in numbers that weren't true. That was unethical, and likely in violation of the tax code. Lowering his salary was definitely out of the question, even if that meant no longer classifying his truck and his condo as a business expense. "What do you suggest I do?" Dave said.

Frank folded his hands and rested them on his desk between the stacks of files. "Well, it's kind of a "pay me now or pay me later" situation. If you want to sell, you can either take the offer that's been given, or you can wait. But if you wait, take the time to build your company so that it's worth the valuation you want. It'll take patience, though, and work, and a team."

"Where should I start?"

"That's up to you," Frank said. "I'm certified to advise on the numbers. I'm not certified on management, operations, or sales. That's your department."

"CYA, huh?" Dave said.

Frank shrugged. "Take it or leave it."

A CLOSER LOOK

Sooner or later, a panicked seller will delve into his business numbers. He'll need the assistance of his advisors in those fields. This is often a difficult but necessary conversation. The business seller needs to hear how his financial statements are keeping him from his financial goals. But he also needs to understand that his financial statements are simply a snapshot of current activity. With good planning, the business owner can use them to target better numbers over time as a springboard for growth.

The difficulty, though, remains in how he goes about asking questions, deciding whom he can trust, and working with his employees. A low-valuation offer forces the business seller to make a decision. Either:

1) accept the offer,

2) refuse the offer and look for a new buyer (often leading to the same result as accepting the first offer), or

3) refuse the offer, wait, and make changes to the business.

After days or weeks of getting excited about selling, the decision to wait and change a business is a hard pill to swallow. It's a decision that won't be easy, especially if his ego is high and his family is enthusiastic about the prospect of a windfall. Imagined euphoria is an emotional state that is difficult to overcome. It can take days, weeks, or even months to experience an emotional shift. The business owner and his family may even run through the five stages of grief: denial, anger, bargaining, depression, and acceptance.

How the business owner handles this emotional roller coaster determines his vulnerability. Buyers don't care. In fact, the more emotionally vulnerable the seller is, the better the price is likely to be for the buyer. The buyer likes to deal with an emotional seller. The trick for the seller is to turn the situation around and make the buyer emotional, making the buyer WANT to buy the company because none of the other companies the buyer is looking at are worthy. Owners should aim to build a company that stands out among its peers because buyers have options. But it takes courage, discipline, work, and patience to build a company that attracts a large pool of qualified buyers, all ready to pay full price, some even willing to pay a premium.

DECISION

Dave left Frank Addington's accounting office and walked to his truck. Should he sell his truck? Selling Kathy's car would have to wait. How vulnerable was he? Was everybody out to get him? No, he said. He told himself he was still in control, though he felt less convinced with each passing moment.

What should he do? He bought those books that he was reading, but none of them acknowledged what was becoming an out-of-control situation, and all of them had the fatal flaw of assuming that most small businesses are able to be sold. He had to get a new plan. Get new ideas, but what?

He thought back to all the conversations he had the last several days. He had spoken to many people. Some were helpful, others not. His financial advisor, Richard Momoney, had said something back when they discussed ESOPs. Dave dialed his number.

"Hey, Dave," Richard said. "Good to hear from you. How's the selling process going?"

"Insane. I'm getting all kinds of feedback, but no one seems to have a grip on it."

"Yeah, it can be crazy."

"Hey. Last time we spoke, you suggested a name I may want to call."

"Miagi. Bob Miagi."

"Is he good?"

"Very."

"Can you send me his number?"

"I'll text it to you now."

Dave said thanks and ended the call. While he was driving down the road, a text appeared on Dave's phone with Miagi's number on it.

22
DAY 13 MONDAY
7:45 A.M.

Dave sat at the coffee shop. A muscle-bound guy in a tank top and baseball cap worked at his laptop in a corner table. At another table, a girl with pink hair laughed with another girl about a family mishap. The smell of espresso filled the air. Music played from the overhead speakers.

Dave wasn't keen on meeting in a coffee shop, but it was morning, and that was the first time available. So long as none of his employees walked in and found out he was selling he'd be okay. The music and the noise prohibited any eavesdropping. Better still, it seemed most of the other patrons focused on themselves.

"Mr. Garrity?"

Dave stood to see a slender man with kind features. He was dressed in business casual, wearing a sports coat and holding a black folder. "Mr. Miagi?"

"Yes, sir."

Dave said, "Please," and he beckoned for the man to sit down.

Miagi pulled out a chair and rested his folder on the table. "I'm glad to meet you. When we talked on the phone, you said the sooner the better. I hope this place is okay?"

"It'll work. I don't see anyone here I recognize."

"Yeah, that can be difficult when you're trying to sell. If you're not careful, it's easy to get paranoid."

"Tell me about it."

After a bit of small talk, Miagi leaned forward. "So, tell me what's going on?"

Dave ran down the events of the last two weeks, beginning with the cancer question on his shoulder and how he's still waiting for lab results. He explained how he had hoped Don, his son, would take over the business, but that Don was now moving to Connecticut and taking Dave's grandkids with him. Kathy still didn't like it, but she focused on the prospect of selling. The thought of selling and making a windfall had kept her happy, but that all ended when he received Bill Steele's surprisingly low offer from Conqueror Capital. He and Kathy haven't smiled much the last few days.

Dave also told Bob Miagi how he had met with Frank Addington, and that he questioned why the valuation seemed so low. He also mentioned that he had a friend who was also selling, and how everything worked out for him on the first try. He admitted he felt cheated somehow. He wondered why things couldn't work out for him on the first try, too.

Bob Miagi sat, listening and nodding and letting Dave talk.

Dave told him everything. He felt relieved. Dave said, "So, it's probably the craziest situation you've heard, right?"

Bob shook his head. "No. In fact, it's quite common what you're going through."

"Come on."

"No. Really. Have you seen the numbers?"

"My statements?"

"Not those, no. I mean the numbers for successful business sales?"

"No. I guess I haven't."

"It's not great odds. The fact is that of all businesses that open, only twenty percent of them are put up for sale."

"That's not so bad."

"Perhaps, but only twenty percent of those get sold. Twenty percent of twenty percent. That means only four percent of all business owners reach a deal to sell their business to an outsider."

"I didn't know that. But that four percent must be pretty happy they were able to get a deal done."

"Well, that's where it gets interesting. Surveys of business owners who sell tell a different story. Can you believe only fifty percent of business owners who successfully sell their business are happy when it's all said and done?"

"You're pulling my leg. Why wouldn't a seller be happy?"

"Look at what you've told me. You're pressured because of health concerns. Your son isn't taking over your business as an inside buyer. The ESOP route has its challenges. And you just received a low-ball offer that's less than half of what you had in mind. You wonder if that's all you're going to get, and it scares you. Your choice is either to wait and work while your health is suspect, or to give in and take the lower amount. These buyers are smart. They know your emotions. Many guys in your situation eventually give in, take the offer, and try to eke out a retirement by cutting expenses and living well below your dreams."

Dave leaned back. "I don't like hearing this."

"And I don't like having to put it this way, but unfortunately, too many owners who want to sell make a great outcome less achievable than it could be. That's why I do what I do."

"And what is that?"

Bob Miagi leaned forward. "I'm a Mergers & Acquisitions Advisor and I help guys like you. While you're getting your company ready for sale, I become your coach. You, of course, are the quarterback, but I put a winning team around you to help make sure you succeed. I want your team to be smarter, savvier, and shrewder than the buyer's team. And never forget, the buyer does have a team. You'll eventually find out who his players are and, when you both get on the field, you want to be the winner when the game is finished."

"Sounds good."

"It is. And the end result is that when you know your business is ready to sell, you're more in control of the situation. At least they won't be able to play on your emotions. Instead, they'll see a business that is showing great financial statements and has a great growth story. They'll know if they don't make the right offer, someone else will jump on the opportunity."

"That would be a relief."

"It is. I've seen it time and again. Buyers don't just want a business that can compensate the owner or owners. They want a business that will grow dramatically and appreciate in value, at least the sophisticated buyers do. When you show them that, you'll more likely be in the driver's seat and command a higher price. More than you would have received otherwise."

Dave nodded. He liked what he was hearing. "Okay. So what does it take?"

"Well, three things. Strategy. Time. And money."

"Of course."

"Your team will be made up of service professionals. Some you already may be working with. Others we'll have to evaluate. Perhaps trade for a free agent. But I'm going to be the one that will coordinate the players, making sure the processes are in place to get you closer to what you are looking for, notwithstanding market conditions."

"How long will it take?"

"That depends on the shape your business is in now, the goals you want to achieve, and the gaps in between. But we shorten whatever time it takes by focusing on those high-priority systems first."

"Right. So what are your terms?"

Bob Miagi nodded and opened his black folder. "Yes. Let's get into that."

A CLOSER LOOK

There are different types of service providers (or intermediaries) who assist business sellers. They generally fall into two categories. The first and most common are listing agents, often known as business brokers. They represent a business by listing it on certain websites and listing services for buyers to find. For too many business brokers, it tends to be a numbers game. They'll help a business seller get exposure, but not much more. Unfortunately, they offer minimal value to the business prior to selling.

The other type of intermediary, however, takes a different approach, and they tend to refer to themselves as M&A Advisors. M&A stands for Mergers and Acquisitions. Knowing the dangers of an unsuccessful sale, these advisors typically arrange a team of professionals to assist the business owner in optimization, working to solidify business processes that increase the business value in as short a time as possible.

This doesn't happen in one week or one month and rarely in one year. Sometimes it can take two years or more, depending on the nature of the business and the extent of the "problems" that need to be fixed.

If the owner wants "full price" for the business, he must be proactive. Before they take over, sophisticated buyers will prefer that the problems first be corrected.

A team-oriented approach, however, is highly strategic because it equalizes the closing situation. After all, buyers show up with teams. Why shouldn't the seller?

DECISION

Dave shook hands with Bob Miagi, telling him he'd think of the idea and get back to him. As he climbed into his truck, he remembered what Miagi had said. The idea of having a team on his side of the closing table relieved him. But he would have to pay for the idea. He thought of his company's financial statements, his ratios, and FineLine's growth story. Could his ratios improve if he was spending money on optimization? Was he going to have to sell his condo and his truck? No way! Couldn't he optimize the company on his own? After all, he was the boss. He knew his business better than anyone. He was in control. Couldn't he just do things better from this point forward and not have to spend the extra cash?

How it would work having Miagi become his selling consultant? What would happen if an outside consultant suddenly came inside his operations and made directives to his employees? Would they suspect that he was trying to sell, and that's why the consultant was there? It seemed too risky.

Dave wasn't ready to hire a team. He was in control. He could sell his own business. He could regroup and figure it out. He had registered for the seminar suggested to him by Mark Bragowski. That was tomorrow. Maybe there he'd learn the best next steps.

23

DAY 14 TUESDAY

6:30 P.M.

Dave stepped through the elevator doors on the twenty-sixth floor of the Grand Smoke Lounge in Atlanta's Buckhead district. Quiet music played as business professionals in coats and ties sipped their drinks at the lounge or scrolled through their cell phones. They sat in cushioned chairs, chatting about business news and political gossip. The windows were wide and inviting, displaying a view of southern buildings and forests that extended across the horizon. Large cumulus clouds floated overhead and blocked the setting sun where they cast their shadows.

Dave felt nervous. He rarely went downtown except for a client lunch. He felt claustrophobic in the metro area. There were too many people. But he'd endure it this time. He wanted to figure this out. Could the seminar help? Would they provide additional information? Would he be allowed to ask questions? What other business owners there were trying to sell their business? Were they going through the same problems he was? At what stage were they in the process: just thinking about it, or further down the road and finding out it's not so easy? Who else was going to the seminar? Would it be anyone he knew?

Would any of them know him?

His employees were not business owners, though. The likelihood of them coming to this seminar was slim to none. Dave went to the bar where another man was sitting, a glass of wine on the bar in front of him while he scrolled his phone. Dave asked the bartender for a draft beer.

The man looked up from his phone and nodded. "You here for the seminar?"

Dave held his breath, quietly told himself to have courage, and said, "Yeah. I guess you are, too?"

"I am." He held out his hand. "Steve Klewe. I've got a shop on the west side of town."

Dave shook hands. "Nice to meet you. Dave Garrity. I've got a manufacturing plant just outside the perimeter." Dave observed the man and realized they shared many of the same characteristics: gray hair, slightly hunched over, bags under the eyes. This man looked as tired as he was.

"Are you just thinking of selling?" Steve said.

"More so in the past few weeks."

"Me, too." Steve sipped his wine. "It's funny how the years go by while you're running your business. Exiting is always in the back of your mind, but then one day it flies to the forefront like a freight train."

Dave nodded and lifted his beer. "I'll say. How's the process going for you?"

"I haven't started yet. But I can see it coming, so might as well start preparing. You?"

Dave sipped his draft. "Just curious what's all entailed," he lied.

"I imagine it's more than we imagine. These seminars seem to just cover the surface."

"Yeah. Once we're on their list, they are going to swoop in and promise the world."

Steve laughed. "Are you sure you're just curious? Sounds like you're already down this road."

Dave didn't want to show his hand. "Aren't all seminars the same?"

"Yeah, I guess you're right."

The light faded in the faraway horizon as the sun set in the west. Atlanta's city lights sparkled and dotted the countryside.

"What kind of manufacturing do you do?" Steve asked.

"Gears. Mainly parts to help with supply chain operations."

"Interesting," Steve said. "My grandson's baseball coach works for a gear company. I think he's up your way. You don't know a guy by the name of Burke, do you? Tim Burke?"

Dave clenched his jaw. The man next to him just named his operations manager. What in the world? He had been so careful the past several weeks. He didn't want to let his employees know he was thinking of selling, and here he was at a "How to Sell Your Business" seminar and one of the other attendees mentioned his operations manager. By name, no less! He wanted to keep this quiet. He had to. "No. Doesn't ring a bell," Dave said.

"He must work somewhere else."

Dave had to change the subject. "What kind of a shop do you run?"

"HVAC. Been doing that a long time."

Suddenly, a woman walked up to Dave and Steve. "Hello, Gentlemen. If you're here for the seminar on selling your business, it's about to start. The room is past the elevators, to the right, and you'll see the room on your left."

Dave and Steve thanked the woman. "I'll see you inside," Dave said, trying to distance himself from the informant.

Dave left the man, trying to keep from shaking from worry.

A CLOSER LOOK

Many brokers and companies have adopted the popular method of seminars to attract prospects. It's no different with seminars in the business selling arena. Seminars are designed to attract, gather information, and build relationships with potential prospects in exchange for strategic information presented in a group setting. This format allows for networking, shared discussion, and question-and-answer sessions that often yield faster and more comprehensive information than the business seller may acquire on his own.

The information presented in seminar presentations remains general, however, because it's difficult to design a presentation made for all types of businesses facing all kinds of issues. As noted before, every business is different, and every business owner, while often sharing similar characteristics with each other, is also different in his financial goals, business challenges, markets, etc. The best an attendee can do at a presentation is to raise his hand and ask specific questions pertaining to his own business, allowing the other attendees to listen and learn. It's also possible for the attendee to learn an answer to a question he may not have thought to ask if another attendee raises his hand.

Seminars, however, are still just a marketing tool. While they will relay information, when the seminar is finished, the business seller remains on his own to do everything himself unless he decides to hire the seminar experts for his particular situation. The seminar providers hope that by inviting multiple people, some will decide to hire them.

The seminar information will have its limitations. At the end of the day, the business owner must decide how he will proceed to make a successful sale. Will he do it on his own or will he not? If not, who will he use to help him? If a business seller attends a seminar, these are really the questions he's trying to answer.

Also, seminars for business sellers remain in a group setting. While chances are low that an employee will discover a business owner's intent to sell from a seminar, the fact is other people will be there, and it's always possible for word to spread if one isn't careful.

DECISION

Dave hurried out of the seminar, trying to avoid eye contact with Steve. His heart raced as he found his truck in the parking garage. What was he to do? Should he call Tim Burke? No way. He denied that he knew him, but what if they talked? What if Steve described him? As he climbed into the truck, he felt everything slipping away. His business was good, but his future was uncertain. His future would be more uncertain if his business suddenly had employee issues.

He couldn't let it happen. He had to think but as he drove outbound along the Atlanta streets to make his way home, he struggled to think. What would he do? How would he proceed? He couldn't let word spread, because then the whole thing could fall apart.

He had to remain in control. He didn't want to do it, but what choice did he have? If his employees challenged him about selling, he would have to lie.

24
DAY 15 WEDNESDAY
9:00 A.M.

Dave called a meeting with his employees and sat in the FineLine Manufacturing conference room. Diane appeared with her notebook and pen in hand. Ava, his receptionist, remained at her desk answering the phone. He smiled at Diane. He was in control. He was going to do what he had done for years. Take charge! His aim for this meeting was to establish some new parameters and organize his internal team to increase revenues and decrease costs. They were going to make some changes. Who were Frank Addington and Bill Steele and Max Hatchet anyway? Numbers guys? Come on. Dave had built a business of people. It generated cash. Any business buyer worth his salt would know it was worth at least $10 million, twelve if there was an earnout and Dave stayed on a year or more to help with the transition.

Diane sat at the table. Her face was stern and focused, as always.

"You good, Diane?"

"I'm ready."

"That's what I like to hear," Dave said. Some of his old energy was returning. This is good, he thought.

Cliff Walden, FineLine Manufacturing's warehouse supervisor, entered the room. After getting a cup of coffee, he sat down, his hands folded across his lap. "Everything alright?" Dave said.

"Yeah. Just thinking."

Tim Burke walked into the room. He said hello to Diane, Cliff, and Dave. When he made eye contact with Dave, however, Tim quickly pulled his eyes away.

Dave said, "Tim, you ready to go?"

Tim said, "Yeah." It wasn't the "Yes, sir," response he usually gave.

Did Steve get a hold of Tim last night? Dave couldn't let it go. He had to know. "Are you okay?"

"Yes, sir."

What did that mean? Was he patronizing him? Was he not? He couldn't tell. "Alright," Dave said. "Everyone's here. I called this meeting because I've been going through some numbers lately, and with the confusion we're having with CWB, I want us to have a plan. It's in our best interests to keep the processes running, and I want to be certain we have no gaps in our systems."

Tim cleared his throat and looked at Cliff, but Cliff sat, waiting.

"Okay," Dave said. "CWB is our biggest customer. They make up about twenty-five percent of our business. A few weeks ago, they put a bid out for some three-fifths gears. We usually hear from them in about two weeks, so we should hear from them any day now. Are we ready to handle the orders when they come in?"

Tim and Cliff eyed each other again, neither speaking.

"What is it?" Dave said.

Cliff leaned forward. "Diane, we got that fax from CWB issuing the correction last week, right?"

"We did. I have it on my desk."

Cliff nodded.

"Why?" Dave said.

"Well, I talk with Larry at CWB every few days as part of my SOPs - he's their warehouse manager. You know, to make sure things are okay and we're doing a good job from his end."

"What's he saying?" Dave said.

"Well, I just get the feeling that they are having issues."

"Maybe. But that can be our opportunity. If we make sure we remain a part of their solutions, we'll help pull them out of whatever they're going through and we'll have a customer for life. Now, things are going smoothly with Aerolift, right?"

His managers nodded.

"Great, is there anything we need to do differently than what we're doing?"

Tim said, "So long as the supplies come in on time, we're able to deliver, and we have been delivering."

"That's good," Diane said. "CWB is worth a lot, and I don't want to remind everybody how much their business means to us."

"I agree," Dave said. "All the same, let's each come up with ideas on where we can improve. Let's meet here tomorrow morning, same time. I want all of us to bring ten ideas on what we can do to take care of them, and what we can do when we win their bid."

His managers nodded their heads. Dave excused them from the room, feeling like the man in control he had always been.

After Diane and Cliff exited the conference room, Tim stopped. He turned around. "Boss, can I ask you a question?"

Dave's heart skipped a beat. "Yea. Sure. Anything."

"I don't know how to ask you this, but are you selling your business?"

Dave blinked, then chuckled to hide his terror. "No. What gave you that idea?"

"There's been some whispers. I figured I'd come right out and ask."

"Whispers?"

"You've just been acting strange."

Dave had to deflect. Anything to convince Tim he wasn't selling. "There has been something. I had a skin diagnosis. There's a fifty-fifty chance it's cancer, but the lab results haven't come back yet."

"I'm sorry to hear that."

"The good news is the doc thinks a worst-case scenario is treatable."

"That's good."

"That's why I've been acting the way I have."

Tim held his mouth tight.

"What?" Dave said.

"Nothing. Just let me know how I can help." Tim left the room and went to his office.

Dave, now alone in the conference room, slumped his shoulders and rested his palms on the table.

A CLOSER LOOK

It's going to happen. At some point, the business owner's employees will learn of a sale, either after or before it happens. If an owner is able to keep things secret, his announcement will be a shock to his staff. He wants to keep it a secret because the buyer will want the staff to remain and keep operations going.

If employees bail, either before or after the sale, there can be problems with the contract terms. The company's performance may also suffer, leaving the business seller's financial situation in doubt.

Before the sale, however, there are other challenges. People are observant. They whisper around the water cooler. They discuss among themselves what they think is happening. If there is any rumor of a potential business sale, they will talk.

The question becomes, at what point does an employee act negatively to the possibility of a business sale? What are the ways an employee can act negatively? The list can include many behaviors, such as underperformance of job responsibilities, quiet quitting, spreading gossip that can reach the ears of customers and suppliers, or resigning altogether and leaving for a competitor.

As to when these behaviors appear is a question of morale. Uncertainty affects morale. A leader doesn't have to announce he is leaving. Simple rumors of his departure cause major uncertainty within the minds of employees. How they react becomes a fight against human nature, and human nature can be difficult to overcome.

A business owner would best devise a plan to tell his employees. Exactly how will he let them know? When will he let them know? Who will he let know? What will he say when he lets them know? In addition to a plan, he'll also want to consider contingency plans. What will he do if a rumor begins that he is selling? How will he answer that? How will he act? What will he say? When will he say it? Telling his employees isn't usually a checklist item in a business owner's exit strategy, but it must be. It must be a thoroughly-vetted strategy laid out with alternative courses of action based on changing circumstances.

DECISION

As good as Dave felt beginning the meeting, he suddenly felt tired. Running the business was wearing on him, and he knew it. He remembered the words of Bob Miagi, that buyers were patient. He remembered Kathy's words to him, that he was in control, and he could do this. He didn't know exactly how he would succeed, but he knew he had to believe he would. He raised himself up. He pounded the conference table with his fist. "I am in control. I will win!" he said.

25
DAY 15 WEDNESDAY
9:35 A.M.

Cliff's concern about CWB bothered Dave. He sat in his office chair. His mind flipped from self-comforting statements of confidence to fears of doubt. He was going to win and sell his business. But what if CWB left? He was better than Mark Bragowski. But Dave knew he did not even have a legitimate offer. Dave told himself he was a superb businessman, bringing in cash flow for his family. But his accountant had told him several of his ratios were off. He went back and forth in his mind. It was driving him crazy.

He wanted to focus. He had to give himself an assignment, any assignment. He wrote down his ten ideas to help CWB. He could offer a free evaluation of their business, and check to see if FineLine Manufacturing should research and develop a proprietary gear designed specifically for CWB. He could build a better relationship, perhaps taking Marge Magnum out to lunch and getting to know her and her business operations more. He could assist CWB's marketing program, ensuring that their messaging included FineLine Manufacturing gear specs and helping solidify the intertwining of their business relationship. Heck, maybe he could offer her use of his beach condo in Destin. That's what it was for. Wasn't it? To build client relationships?

As the ideas flowed, Dave was gaining more confidence. It's always better to focus on the task at hand than the chaos all around you, he told himself. Work makes the world go around.

Dave's cell phone rang. His heart skipped a beat. Was it good news? Were the lab results back in? Was it Mark Bragowski calling to entice him to spend money he hadn't made yet? Then again. . .

He picked up the phone. "This is Dave."

"Dave, Bill Steele. How are you doing?"

Dave checked to make sure the office door was closed. He leaned back in his seat. He had to play it cool. Figure out if there was a way to raise their offer. "Good to hear from you."

"We haven't heard from your side since we sent you the letter of intent."

"I'm sorry. I've just been busy."

"You'll be a lot less busy if you take the offer."

Dave nodded. This guy was good. With everything going on in Dave's life, he could accept the offer and transition into retirement. Except for one thing. "I have to tell you, Bill. I was hoping for a lot more than the offer you made."

"I understand," Bill said. "We hear that all the time. But the numbers you gave us initially say otherwise. In fact, based on those, we were generous by going above the market value."

Dave held the phone away from his ear. Did the guy really just say he was being generous? "I just think it's worth a lot more."

"Based on what, Dave?" Bill said. "Blood, sweat, and tears? Hey, I work hard, too. I get that. If I put all that effort in to build a business, of course I'd want my payday. But the market doesn't work that way, unfortunately. It can be unfair. Supply and demand drive prices. You know that, Dave. You're a reasonable businessman. You've been smart to build a great cash-flow operation. But the market drives prices, and right now you don't have any other offers. Am I right?"

Dave put his elbows on his desk and closed his eyes while he held the phone to his ear. No, he didn't have any other offers. Yes, he was getting tired. Yes, his health was suspect. Yes, his accountant's value estimate aligned with the buyer's. Geez. Was there no way out? Was he being constricted by some invisible anaconda and he didn't even know it until it was too late? "I've got some prospects," Dave said. He still wasn't comfortable lying.

"That's great," Bill said. "Well, listen. If they work out for you, terrific. I'll be glad to hear it. But just know this. We're still interested in your business, but we'll likely reduce our offer for each negative thing we find in due diligence. And remember, we haven't even started that yet. Just keep that in mind as you think about the price we've talked about so far."

"You are a shark, aren't you?"

"No. Just a guy who knows what he wants."

Dave's face turned red. He hung up the phone. He didn't even say goodbye. Who the hell did Bill Steele think he was!

A CLOSER LOOK

A business offer in hand remains just an offer until the final documents are signed by both parties. While the business seller is happy to receive an offer, the game isn't over once the offer is received. In fact, the game has elevated to another level of intensity.

It's difficult to imagine that a buyer might make an initial offer, only to make a lower offer later, but that's what many do. It's a psychological strategy that puts pressure on the seller, forcing his hand either to get a better offer from someone else or to watch his property lower in value. Why does this work? Because, unlike public companies whose stock trades and fluctuates with the market every day, business owners don't see their business value swing in intra-day trading. The business owner pictures a value in his mind, often for years, without considering what a buyer would pay for it. Eventually, the business owner has imagined a business's valuation number so often it becomes second nature to him, almost like reality.

And that is exactly what the buyer wants to happen. When the buyer suddenly comes along and suggests lowering his imagined valuation for each negative thing found during due diligence, the business owner begins feeling pressure. The seller is now hearing from a buyer that his own company is becoming devalued. Unless another buyer enters the picture, the market is now driving his business's price lower, and the temptation arises to panic-sell by accepting the offer before the price falls to rock bottom.

It's a clever trick, one that buyers practice regularly. But the seller can overcome it by remembering one thing: there is no real value in a business until it's actually been sold. If a buyer doesn't want to see his business's valuation drop, he can stop communications with the manipulative buyer, return to work on his business, and increase the valuation to get the offer he desires.

This is easier said than done, of course, but it is something to keep in mind when negotiations ratchet up to higher levels.

DECISION

Dave's face remained red. He had to calm down. He wanted to blow off steam. He hadn't been to the gym in a while. He decided to run to the gym for lunch. He needed to throw some weight around before he punched a hole in his office wall.

26
DAY 15 WEDNESDAY
6:15 P.M.

Dave pulled his truck into the large garage and walked into the kitchen. Bernie, his Saint Bernard, lumbered up to Dave, his tongue hanging out and his bushy tail dusting the nearby cabinet doors. Dave leaned down to hug Bernie. Bernie slobbered a giant lick on Dave's cheek. "Hey, boy. Glad to see you."

"You're home," Kathy said. She was sitting on the den sofa. Dave raised himself to see his wife scrolling through her phone while watching the news.

Dave approached Kathy and bent down to kiss her forehead. He was feeling better after spending some time at the gym. "Hi, honey. How was your day?"

She didn't look up. She scrolled some more on her phone.

"What are you looking at?" Dave said.

She put the phone down. "I've been thinking. Maybe we should take that offer."

"What?"

"You'll get the cash. You can spend time on your health. While you're transitioning out, you'll still get a salary for a year. And when it's over you can start another business and do it all over again. Who knows, maybe we'll make a fortune with thoroughbreds."

"I'm going to be seventy in a few years. Who's to say I'll be able to, or want to, do it all over again?"

"You can do anything you set your mind to," Kathy said.

"When did you change your mind?"

"I've just been thinking. Have you talked with Mark?"

"Not since last week. Why?"

"I haven't talked with Melissa, either. They're probably too snobbish now that they've got their windfall."

"They're our friends."

"Maybe."

"Let's not judge until we hear from them."

"We were supposed to go with them to look at horses. So what happened? Are they too good to take us with them?"

Dave kneeled next to Kathy. "Honey, we're not them. We'll take care of ourselves. We always have. Remember?"

"That's right," Kathy said. "You should call that New York company and accept their offer."

"I don't want to do business with them."

Kathy's eyes grew wide. "What?"

"They're sharks. They said they're already offering above market and, as I've come to learn, they'll just keep lowering their offer with the more things they find that they don't like."

"So we take the offer today."

"I hung up on the guy."

"You what?"

"I hung up on him."

"Well, call him back. Apologize."

"I don't want to do that," Dave said.

"Dave, you don't have any other offers."

"No, but–."

"So, take their offer."

"Why are you in such a hurry?"

"Dammit, Dave. Take the money!"

Bernie left the living room and hid behind the kitchen table.

Dave grabbed the back of the sofa with his hand. "Hold on. It's my business."

"It's our business. I helped you all these years."

"Yes, and–."

"And we're in this together."

"But that doesn't mean we're selling, at least not to them."

"You're going to screw it up."

"How do you know?"

"Because you don't know what you're doing. You don't have a plan. You go to seminars in the evening and meet with strangers at coffee shops. You have books you haven't read yet. And you've got lab tests that are yet to come in, and I don't know what's going to happen to us!" Kathy's eyes turned red and filled with tears.

Dave leaned in and hugged Kathy.

"Don't touch me," Kathy said.

"I'll figure this out. I am figuring this out."

Kathy stood up and left the sofa. She picked up her phone. "I'm not hungry. Fix yourself something to eat." She left him kneeling in the den while she marched up the steps. Her feet stomped over the upstairs carpet, and the bedroom door slammed shut.

Dave looked at Bernie. Bernie remained hidden behind the kitchen table and chairs. The dog raised his bushy eyebrows.

"I guess it's just you and me tonight," Dave said.

Bernie whined.

A CLOSER LOOK

The stress of selling can cause a breakdown in communication if it's not handled well from the outset. The problem is no one knows what will happen because the selling party cannot control the actions of the buyers. If he fails to talk with his family members, however, it will only add to the stress and confusion. This will make their situation even weaker in a business selling scenario.

In Dave's situation, he let his circumstances dictate his thoughts rather than forming a plan to achieve what he wanted. There's a big difference between the owner having their plan and having someone else's plan, and believing he's in control is often the very thing that creates this vulnerability. He believes he can juggle all the nuanced balls of selling a business until he eventually drops one. At that point, all the balls come crashing down, and the situation becomes worse than before he considered selling. That same optimism, independence, and desire for control that sustained him all these years is now hindering him at this critical point in his life.

A business seller would do better to sit down with his family from the outset and discuss what is going on rather than allow questions and hopes and fears to dictate the selling family's emotions. Every seller should remember: the higher their emotions become, the more vulnerable they are to the whims of the buyer.

DECISION

Dave lay on the sofa, flipping the TV's channels with the remote. First, there was news, but that depressed him. Then there was sports, but that wasn't reality. Then there was a movie on, but that also wasn't reality. Wanting something tangible, he flipped the channels.

Bernie walked up to him and licked his face. Dave patted the dog and told him to lie down on the rug. After a few moments, Bernie circled and dropped to the floor. He rested his head on his paws. The dog raised his eyebrows as he watched Dave handle the remote.

Dave flipped the channels, but questions ran through his mind. What was he going to do? He wanted to be his wife's hero, but she was losing it. If he took the offer, he'd collect $4 million, but he could make the company more valuable than that. He just knew it. And what about the lab tests? When were those going to come back at him? Did he have cancer? If so, how aggressive was it? And what if he did wait to sell? Could he convince Kathy that patience would pay out? But how much patience? It didn't help that Mark and Melissa had sold and suggested all sorts of things like racehorses and trips to Italy. It was interesting that Mark and Melissa had become quiet since their sale. Probably celebrating and working out the transition details, Dave thought.

Dave decided to take stock of where he was. He had a purchase offer. That was a good thing. Maybe if he called Bill Steele tomorrow he could talk him into going easy during the due diligence. Nah, probably not. His business was still operating, regardless. If employees whispered that he was selling, maybe now was a time to announce it anyway.

Then again, would he take an $11 million cut for all his years of sweat and toil? Worst case scenario, he could maintain and optimize his business for a future owner. "So long as I keep CWB," he said. It was the last thought he had before he drifted off to sleep.

27
DAY 16 THURSDAY
8:40 A.M.

Dave sat at his office desk. He felt nervous, but after a night on the sofa, he was ready to make a decision. Life happens. Businesses get sold. It happens every day. Why not for him? Why not right now?

He didn't feel great about making the call to Bill Steele. Would Conqueror Capital treat his employees right? Was he settling for the amount they offered? So many questions ran through his mind, but he was tired, and he just had to come to some decision and live with it.

There was a knock. Tim Burke leaned in the doorway. "Are we meeting at nine?"

"You know-."

His phone rang.

"Hold on a second."

Dave picked up the phone. The voice on the other end said, "Mr. Garrity?"

"This is he."

"This is Misty at Dr. Blackwood's office."

"Oh. Could you hold on a second?" Dave motioned for Tim to leave the office and shut the door. Tim obliged, closing the door. Dave, alone in his office, said, "Sorry about that. I'm here."

"Yes. We are calling to let you know that we did get the results from the labs regarding the sample we took from your shoulder. I want to tell you that it did come back positive."

Dave blinked, shocked at the news. "Positive?"

"Yes. There are cancer cells in the sample."

"What does that mean?"

"Dr. Blackwood would like to schedule an appointment with you as soon as you're available. Would you have some time soon?"

Dave noticed his hands were shaking. "Yes. How about this afternoon?"

"Will three o'clock work?"

"Yes. I'll be there then." Dave hung up the phone. Suddenly, he remembered the manager's meeting. It was scheduled in the next twenty minutes. He wasn't up for it right then. He sent an email to his managers, pushing the meeting back until eleven.

He wanted to call Kathy, but he wanted to give her good news, too. After a night on the couch, he just wanted to get things back to normal. He was so stressed, both at work and at home, that he needed to tell her something good. Anything good. If he sold his business and got a check, even if it wasn't for what he hoped for, maybe that would make her happy. First, he would call Bill Steele and get to him before Conqueror Capital sent another email with a reduced offer. He picked up the phone and dialed.

"Steele here."

Who calls himself by his last name? Dave thought. Still, he put on his best smile. "Hi, Bill. This is Dave Garrity."

"Oh. Hi, Dave." Bill's tone was completely different than what he sounded like when they last spoke..

"I've been giving what you said some thought. Quite honestly I thought about it all night. If the initial offer still stands at $4 million, I'll take the offer."

There was a pregnant pause on the other end. Then Bill said, "Dave, I'm sorry to tell you this, but we are rescinding our offer for FineLine Manufacturing."

Dave's shoulders tensed. "You are? Why?"

"We're actually drafting the email now. It'll be in your inbox in the next twenty minutes."

"What happened?"

"Don't lie to me," Bill said. "You know what happened."

"No, I don't."

There was another knock on the door.

"Good luck to you, Dave."

"Bill, I don't—." The line went dead. Dave's forehead suddenly lined with sweat. "What the hell?" Another knock. "What!"

Diane opened the door. She waved a paper in her hand.

"I pushed the meeting back to eleven," Dave said.

"That's not it. We have a problem."

"What now?"

"CWB. They're canceling the contract."

"We've been through this."

"No. This is different. This came from their lawyers." She handed Dave the paper. "They are canceling everything!"

Dave read the fax. It came on legal letterhead; some firm named Rover, Mitchell, & Greene. "Son of a–."

Diane leaned over Dave's desk. "Did you call our lawyers?"

"Yes."

"And?"

"Nothing back yet. I'll call them again right now."

Diane nodded and paced out of Dave's office. Dave sat at his desk. In the last few minutes, he was told he had cancer, he missed out on a $4 million business sale, and he lost his largest customer representing twenty-five percent of his business. He wondered what Bill Steele meant when he accused Dave of knowing.

Did Steele have a connection at CWB? That was it. He had to. Bill had mentioned he noticed some marketing language about FineLine's gears in CWB's marketing. Bill had to have had an inside source at CWB. That's why they rescinded the offer and left the table. Steele knew the fax was coming. The shark was fishing using Dave's own customers!

Dave leaned forward and shook his head. This had turned out to be one hell of a morning. What in the world was he going to say to Kathy?

A CLOSER LOOK

While the risks of selling a business don't often materialize on the same day, they do converge. This is one of the reasons why a business owner selling a business can get caught in his own trap. Health issues aren't stagnant. If they aren't dealt with they can get worse. Market forces aren't stagnant.

They can get worse if the business doesn't adjust. Family pressures aren't stagnant. Communication difficulties can create sleepless nights at home. Selling negotiations aren't stagnant. Buyers know how to play the game, and they will exploit a seller's weaknesses as selling pressures increase. With all these increasing pressures, the business owner will either enlist help or crack under the weight. Buyers know this. One way out of the pressure is for the seller to take the lower offer, and too many sellers take this path to exit.

Then the business seller becomes a part of the fifty percent of sellers who are unhappy after a sale.

Sometimes, however, it takes a disaster for a business owner to relinquish his pride. When a business owner realizes he's not in full control, that's when he's more likely to begin looking for the right kind of help. That's also when he begins looking inward. Selling a business is very personal. It's not an event, it's an experience. Looking at a business sale merely as a transaction diminishes not only the value of the business but also the value of the owner.

While the owner's health and energy may be questionable before he decides to sell, he still has experience and know-how. He just needs to recognize that the business needs to be optimized for a transition. It's like an eagle making sure the chicks can fly on their own once they leave the nest, or like a house that's renovated before being put on the market. A business being sold is the same concept. The business owner, with his ego set aside, should stop thinking of his cash flow as a means to his financial gain, but should now think outwardly toward his business as an entity that will fly long after he's gone, the foundation of which he's ready to hand off to its next owner.

That's the mentality a business seller needs. It's a shift in mindset, to one of nurturing, humility, and wisdom. This shift stops being about his control, but rather becomes about legacy and reputation and a business that will serve others for years to come.

When disaster strikes, the business seller must strive to make this mindset shift. When he does, he is ready to repair the damage he's done to himself and work toward a future with a team focused on winning.

DECISION

At eleven a.m., Dave stood in the conference room. Diane, Tim, and Cliff sat around the table, their faces downcast with the news of CWB. Dave's breath was labored. He wasn't sure what to say. He had lost all control. Everything was falling apart. Not only did he not have the money from the sale, but now he was to undergo cancer treatment while needing to rebuild his business. Would he take a pay cut? Would all of them? Would he have to fire people? Would he survive his cancer diagnosis? Would Kathy divorce him and remarry someone else who had money? This morning he felt like he still had some fight left in him. Now, he felt empty.

"I want you all to know something," Dave said. "I told Tim this yesterday, but I haven't been myself lately."

The three faces stared at him, waiting for what would exit his mouth next.

"I received word this morning that I have a cancer diagnosis, and I'm meeting with the specialists this afternoon about making a treatment plan."

Diane said, "I'm sorry to hear that."

"Sorry, boss," Cliff said.

"Thanks," Dave said. "But I want you to know whatever I have to go through, FineLine Manufacturing will keep running. This business has had difficult days before. But if we stick together we'll get through it."

"What about CWB?" Diane said. "What did our lawyers say?"

Dave sighed. "There's a clause that states the contract will cease if there is a change in business needs."

"Business needs?" Tim said.

"Change in market conditions, strategic direction, or operational requirements."

"That sounds awfully vague," Cliff said.

"It is, and it's subject to interpretation. So our options are to sue them, in which case we'll probably lose and give all our money to the lawyers, or we can move on and grow from this."

"But they're twenty-five percent of our business," Diane said.

"That's a big cut," Tim said.

Dave nodded. "Yes, but what choice do we have?"

28
DAY 16 THURSDAY
3:25 P.M.

The room was sterile, as doctor's offices often are. Dave was cold. His shirt was off. He looked down. His stomach appeared to have grown in just a few weeks. With the added stress, he had been eating more than usual, snacking between meetings, and sitting on his recliner too much.

"Keep still for just a few more minutes," Dr. Blackwood said.

Dave took a deep breath. He sat on the metal table while Dr. Blackwood examined his shoulder.

"Yeah, I can see now why the lab results came back positive," Dr. Blackwood said.

"Has there been any change since I was here last?"

"Not really, but the lab did a good job identifying what's going on with those questionable areas. New information helps a lot. Adds some clarity." Blackwood stood up and wrote some notes on his clipboard. "You can put your shirt back on."

Dave slid his shirt over his head. He was eager to cover himself. "What is the plan?"

Blackwood pulled up a stool and sat in front of Dave. He tapped his pen onto his clipboard. "Two things for sure: surgery and radiation. We'll want to cut out the cancer cells and surrounding tissue to make sure we get it all. After that, we'll want to use radiation, just to make sure there are no bad cells hiding anywhere that we may have missed. Of course, we'll want ongoing examinations. Immunotherapy and targeted therapy may also be considered."

"What are those therapies again?"

"Immunotherapy. We supply you with some drugs that will help boost your immune system so your body can fight the cancer. The targeted therapy consists of specific drugs used to attack melanoma cells. I'm going to do a deeper analysis of the lab results, though, so you can determine if that's what you want to do."

"No chemo?"

"Only if the other treatments don't work. I'd prefer we stay strategic rather than blast you with too many side effects."

Dave nodded. He was glad to have a doctor on his side who appeared to have his best interest at heart. He was thankful to have Dr. Blackwood on his healthcare team. If he had to fight the cancer on his own, he wouldn't survive. He felt completely low. Weak. He was not sure what to think. A few weeks ago he was enjoying life, bragging about his truck and his business at networking breakfasts. Today, he was feeling like an old man. "How long will all this take?"

"The surgery won't take long, just a few hours. You'll be left with a hefty scar, though, and you'll need pain medication for a week or two. As for the radiation, plan on four to six weeks. The procedures only take a minute or two, but we'll want to space them out."

Dave thanked Dr. Blackwood, scheduled his surgery at the front desk, and climbed into his truck. When he turned on the engine, 1980s rock played through the speakers, but he just couldn't listen. He turned the radio off and sat in his truck. He heard his breath. He felt out of shape. He felt his heartbeat inside his chest. He listened to the silence. Outside, the breeze was gently blowing the tree leaves. Birds chirped in the landscape all around him. A car drove on the road behind him. Another much older patient walked into the building, assisted by a family member. He hoped that wouldn't be him one day, but didn't that eventually happen to everybody?

He picked up his phone and was about to dial Kathy's number, but he couldn't bring himself to call. He was thinking of what a fool he had been. Had he found the help he needed earlier, perhaps he would have avoided all of this. Now, his health was in question. His business was in shambles. Anxiety filled his home. What was he going to do? He didn't know. He wanted to call Kathy, but he couldn't admit he had made a mistake. Alone in his truck, he set his cell phone down, leaned his head forward onto the steering wheel, and let the tears flow.

A CLOSER LOOK

The experience of selling a business is highly emotional, full of highs and lows. Make no mistake: if the process isn't managed right, tears will eventually flow after the initial shock ends and disappointment sets in. That's why so few business owners reach the "happy two percent" after selling their business. That means the other ninety-eight percent of business owners fail to make it to the Promised Land. Tears can and do flow.

Selling a business is about so much more than the money. The money acquired from a business sale is a by-product of all the systems of cause and effect that the business owner establishes within his operations. This is a combination of people, processes, and products. While building these systems, however, money can do strange things to people. It can make them lose their way, and lose their focus. The lure of excess cash flow while running his business can blind a business owner from the need to formalize his systems and optimize his business for the next owner.

As mentioned earlier, business valuations aren't recorded every day. How does a business owner know what his business is worth week after week? Or even year after year? How can he see his valuation trends without paying for valuation experts to keep track?

He can't.

That's why it's easy for him to become comfortable with his current cash flow. He'll see those numbers and tell himself he's doing a good job. But he needs to do more. He needs to work beyond his current cash flow to optimize his business for a potential sale. That sale may not be tomorrow. But it will come one day if he's prepared. Remember, business owners will eventually exit their companies. It's just a question of when and how successfully.

It's much better to prepare for a business sale years before an owner's retirement age, long before any health concerns arise, market conditions change, and conditions exist for buyers to pressure the owner.

The struggle is real. So are the emotions. Unprepared business sellers will experience them. Humility and preparation will determine if he overcomes them.

DECISION

Dave lifted his head and wiped the tears from his eyes. He hadn't been scared in a long time, but he was scared now. He had to admit it. He was tired of the stress at home. He was tired of the stress at work. He was tired of the confusion and the uncertainty. And he was tired of being tired.

He imagined Kathy was feeling the same way. He didn't know what she would say, but he loved his wife, and he wanted to talk with her. His phone lay on the passenger seat next to him. He picked it up and called Kathy's number. She didn't pick up. It went to voicemail. "Hi, honey. I'm leaving the doctor's office. I just wanted to let you know I'm coming home."

29
DAY 16 THURSDAY
5:45 P.M.

Dave walked into the kitchen. Kathy was sitting on the sofa. The weatherman was on the TV, showing how storms were brewing and would likely show up in the middle of the night. Bernie walked up to Dave, wagging his large bushy tail. Dave patted his dog's head, and Bernie grinned the way Saint Bernards grin.

As Dave walked over to Kathy, Bernie stood still not knowing what would happen next. He moved behind the kitchen table and sat in the corner. Kathy's eyes were red. She looked angry.

"Hey," Dave said.

"How'd the doctor's visit go?"

"I have to have surgery."

Kathy took a deep breath and let it out. "I'm sorry," she said, mechanically.

"I'll be alright."

"Did you take the offer?"

"No."

Kathy leaned forward and put her face in her hands. "Oh, no."

"Look," Dave said. "I just want to say I'm sorry."

"You've got to fix this."

"That's why I'm here."

"Melissa and Mark–."

"Will you stop it with the Bragowskis. We're not them."

"I'll say."

"My job isn't to keep up with Mark. My job is to take care of us."

"How are you going to do that with cancer?"

Dave felt his face beginning to turn red, but he wasn't going to let that happen. He took a deep breath and waited.

"Well?" Kathy said.

"I have a treatment plan. I have to undergo surgery and four to six weeks of radiation."

"What kind of surgery?"

"The doc said it would only take a few hours. They have to cut out the cancer, and then zap me with radiation treatments to make sure they got it all."

Kathy leaned forward again. "What are we going to do?"

"I'm not dead."

"But what happens to our money?"

Dave stopped short of telling her about CWB. "I have a business to run."

"How can you run a business if you've got cancer?"

Dave knelt next to his wife. Her eyes were wide with fear. "Honey, it'll be alright."

"But what about Italy–?"

"Will you stop thinking of yourself for a change?"

Kathy raised her head.

Dave struggled to keep his head low. "I don't care about Italy, or horses, or the Bragowskis. All I care about is us. You, me, and our family."

"But Don is moving to Connecticut and taking my grandkids away–."

"Good for him. We did our job well. He's got a great opportunity. But he's no longer us. You and I have to evaluate our own situation and set things right for us."

Kathy leaned back. "So, what are you going to do?"

"First of all, admit I need help."

"But you're in control."

"This is a different game, Kathy. I need to do something I don't want to do."

"What's that?"

"Hire the right help. These buyers have a team. It's about time we have a team, too."

"But that will cost money."

"All good investments do."

A CLOSER LOOK

Sometimes people have to hit rock bottom before they admit they need to change, and that happens quite often in the business selling process. The purpose of this book is to take you, the reader, into that common emotional experience through Dave's story so you'll understand what rock bottom feels like before you reach a real selling scenario yourself. I also didn't want you to have the disastrous misfortune of financial difficulties and emotional trauma, and ultimately regret, that can come with mismanaging a business sale.

Remember, though, how only twenty percent of all businesses that list for sale get sold? The vast majority of those eighty percent that don't sell simply close shop, leaving the business owner in a predicament where he has to either find new employment in his old age or live off what he was able to save from his personal salary, distributions, and possibly retirement plans.

Many business owners give up and choose to close shop. Remember, only four percent of businesses sell. The rest remain listed, and that is if they are listed at all.

Fortunately, there is another option. If a business is still operational, there will be an opportunity to find the right kind of help - a knowledgeable M&A advisor who knows how to put together a winning team that optimizes the business for a sale, a team that encourages buyers to make higher offers than they would have made otherwise.

Not all business sellers will make this choice, but those who do must be ready for the resulting changes suggested by the team. With the right attitude and perspective, a business seller can build a team that enters the negotiation field of play and wins handsomely with a check at closing. There will still be back and forth in the negotiations, and not all deals will be perfect, but with the team-oriented exit strategy, the business seller has a much higher chance at success than if he were to do it on his own. He'll also want to avoid hiring a business broker who's only going to list the business without any additional value or services.

DECISION

Kathy said, "Who's going to be on your team?"

"Our team," Dave said. "This isn't just me. This is about both of us. I'm going to do a better job of communicating with you about what we're doing."

"But, we've been doing that."

"No, we haven't. I've been uncomfortable with all the talk about Italy and thoroughbreds before I had an offer."

Kathy nodded. "That put a lot of pressure on you, didn't it?"

Dave nodded. "Yeah. That and the cancer question."

"I'm sure the Bragowski's selling didn't help, either."

"No."

"And I guess I was too upset about Don moving the grandkids away. I put all my focus on retirement to distract me from that."

"I'm sorry," Dave said.

"Me, too."

"Well, let's start over. Let's start by getting the right people on the bus."

"Who's that?"

"First, I'm calling Bob Miagi."

"The guy from the coffee shop?"

"Yeah, the M&A Advisor. He had some good things to say, but at the time we met I wasn't ready to hear them. I think that time is now."

Bernie walked over between Dave and Kathy, wagging his tail. The two of them petted Bernie together while the dog's tongue hung out of his large, smiling mouth.

"You sure it's not too late?" Kathy said.

"It's never too late to do the right thing," Dave said.

30
DAY 17 FRIDAY
7:35 A.M.

Dave sat at the coffee shop. It was his first time back since he last met with Bob Miagi. The atmosphere was lively and energetic as music echoed from the overhead speakers and the aroma of coffee filled the air. The muscle-bound guy wasn't there this time. He was replaced by a young woman wearing glasses and typing on her laptop. The pink-haired lady and her friend were also gone, replaced by two guys in their mid-twenties playing chess.

Bob Miagi walked through the doors, bought himself a coffee, and sat down, placing his black folder on the table.

Dave sipped his coffee. He took it black. After last week's debacles, he didn't feel like spending lavishly, even if it meant cream and sugar in his coffee. "How are you doing?" Dave said.

Bob nodded. "Good. I'm glad you called. I've been thinking about your situation."

Dave shook his head. "You know, when I came down with cancer, I had to rely on a team of doctors for my health. But I was too stubborn to take the same approach with my business. I should've listened to you before. I'm sorry I didn't."

"A friend of mine once said, "You either have a great time or a great story." Either way you come out ahead."

Dave chuckled. "Oh, it's a story alright."

"Tell me what's going on."

Dave sipped his coffee and told Bob about the complete debacle. He explained how he received his cancer diagnosis and was scheduling surgery and radiation treatments. He explained Conqueror Capital's strategy and tactics, and how they worked hard to pressure him. He explained Frank Addington's analysis. He explained how he was about to take Bill Steele's offer, even though it was far below what he wanted. He explained how he lost CWB and twenty-five percent of his revenue. And he explained how he had to talk with his wife, Kathy, and forgive her and himself for being so thick-headed.

Bob nodded. His face was kind and understanding. "And so you didn't sign an NDA with Conqueror Capital before discussing terms with them?"

Dave lowered his head. "I never thought about it."

"How do you feel now?"

"Like an idiot. Scared."

"That's normal."

"But normal doesn't help. I need to fix this."

Bob raised his eyebrows, his face shining with hope. "It can be done. We're going to have our work cut out for us, though."

Dave clasped his coffee cup in his hands. He felt like such a moron. How did all this happen to him?

Before Dave could drift into self-pity, Bob said, "Look, these things happen. But they don't have to stay that way."

"So, what do we do?"

"We do a dive into the company. First, establish your team. We'll break your team into two categories."

"Which are. . .?"

"The first category is your core team. These are your All-Stars, the ones we absolutely have to have. They'll have experience with business transactions, and everything they do will be geared to help you win at the closing."

"So, who are my All-Stars?"

"They are professionals who comprise several disciplines. First, we need someone strong in tax situations. Typically we'll get a CPA for this role. Not all CPAs are created equal, though. We'll need to evaluate his ability to shift."

"What do you mean by shifting?" Dave said.

"Where most business owners get into trouble is they tell their CPA to throw all their toys into the business so it reduces their taxes. Boats, trucks, beach condos. Those sorts of things. We'll need to make sure your CPA understands that when the business gets closer to a sale, the owner would be wise to keep those items off the tax returns and financial statements."

"But don't most business owners run personal items in the business?" Dave said.

"For personal cash flow, it depends. But buyers don't like seeing that. In fact, it can be a deterrent, and I've never seen it where these so-called add-backs make a buyer more comfortable."

"Why?"

"Because it doesn't tell an accurate story of how the company is performing, and because of the banks."

"The banks?"

"Yes. If there's going to be borrowing involved, banks will look at those tax returns. If the returns don't match up nicely with the financial statements, there will be problems. If a business owner runs several personal expenses through the business, they shouldn't expect a buyer to be able to borrow a lot of money from the bank."

"I'm not sure I understand."

"Lots of business owners use their toys to attract clients, thinking it establishes relationships. Or they even do it because they think they're entitled to it. CPAs are often pressured to classify the owner's boats, condos, trucks, and other property as a business expense so that the business is tax efficient. But when those toys are divested at the business sale, exactly what is the business-client relationship built upon? Is it the quality of the product or service? The unique selling proposition? Or is it the condo and the beach?"

"Now wait a minute. We offer a great product," Dave said.

"I'm sure you do, but your competition is catching up. Whether you like it or not, CWB just took away twenty-five percent of your business and gave it to a competitor."

Dave blinked. Miagi's truth hurt.

"Think like a buyer for a minute," Miagi said. "Might the buyer lose a customer after the sale because the relationship was built on toys and the connection with you, and not entirely on the solution to the customer's problem? Would they devalue your business because it's too dependent on you? If that's a possibility, why would a buyer take that sort of risk? Why would he borrow a lot of money to buy a customer base he may lose once the seller takes back his beach condo?"

"I see your point," Dave said. He pictured his truck and his condo. He had pressured Frank Addington to classify them as business expenses years ago. He had considered bribing Marge Magnum to use his beach condo to keep CWB. As much as Dave didn't like hearing it, Bob Miagi was making sense. Dave was beginning to think of his business in a new light. He was beginning to see it from a buyer's point of view.

"I already have a CPA. Can I use him?" Dave asked.

"Maybe. Maybe not. There's a joke in my industry that says 'CPA' actually stands for the most Cautious People Alive. Do you think he's too cautious?"

"I'd say he's been accurate."

"Good. We'll go meet with him together and come to a conclusion."

Dave's thoughts ran. There was so much to consider. He thought of several more questions. "Who else is on our team?"

"Another player we might need is an outsourced CFO," Miagi said.

"What is that?"

"It's a fractional Chief Financial Officer who has worked for at least one company as the head of finance before, either as an employee or an independent contractor. What's most valuable is that he has probably experienced a business transaction personally. He may or may not have direct experience in your industry (preferably he will), but he has seen businesses like yours go through this process."

"I didn't know there were professionals like that."

"There are. And if you look at their online bios, you'll see that they have multiple projects that are either completed or ongoing. They do this sort of thing all the time. They can handle your business's financials, and possibly operations, to help prepare it for sale."

"So, two finance professionals. Is that all?"

"No. You'll also need a transactional business attorney. This is someone who has experience handling an actual business closing and all the legal documents that precede it."

"I know a guy in my breakfast club who's a real estate attorney. He does a lot of closings. Would he be able to do it?"

"Let me put it this way. While a transactional business attorney may be able to handle a real estate closing, you'll want someone who has extensive experience with business closings because they are two completely different animals. Not all real estate attorneys have the experience of handling a business transaction, and because a business transaction is so particular, you'll want an attorney with extensive knowledge to assist you at the closing table."

"So he'll be on my side when we're sitting across the table from the buyers."

"Exactly."

"Okay. So, where do you fit in?"

"Technically, I'm an M&A Advisor, meaning I have extensive experience with mergers and acquisitions. While the players I just mentioned have some experience with business transactions, none of them have dealt with more buyers than I have. It's that experience that will help you think like a buyer, so you can put the pieces in play to gain the greatest advantage for your sale."

"Think like a buyer?"

"Yes. As Sun Tzu says: 'Know thy enemy.'"

"I see. So if those are the All-Stars, what's the other category?"

"The second category is your periphery players. While they might have a limited role in the actual transaction, these players understand that they are not part of the core team. They operate as consultants, optimizing the business in specific areas as needed. These are bankers, property and casualty insurance agents, technical consultants, process consultants, HR consultants, sales and marketing consultants, wealth managers, and any other professionals we deem necessary to optimize your company for a sale."

"That's a lot of people."

"Only if the strategy calls for it. Once we dive into your business, you'll find some of these professionals will be needed more than others. And some may not be needed at all. Regardless, we'll need to make sure that each member of the team, core or periphery, understands their role and when they're needed. It may sound corny and self-evident but we're looking for team-players, people who know when to stay on the bench versus when they're needed on the field. Not everyone has that ability. Ego and the consultant's own cash-flow needs too often get in the way."

Dave imagined all the changes he'd have to make. "How long will it take to fix all this?" he said.

"It's going to take some time, enough so that the financial statements and tax returns show positive trends. But you're looking at many months to a year, if not years."

Years? Dave didn't like the sound of that. He put his elbows on the table and raised his hands to his mouth. His mind swam with thoughts. "What if I don't have years?" he said.

"Well, no offense, but what other options do you have?"

"Fair enough."

Bob leaned forward and slid his black notebook to the side. "Dave, here's the deal. Buyers are becoming more sophisticated. They're all talking about multiples, but that puts you at a disadvantage because multiples may not tell the full story of what a business is worth."

"You know, Conqueror Capital used that term at our meeting. I have to confess I had no idea what they were talking about."

"Of course you didn't. And they knew that. You didn't know what a multiple is, or how to calculate one, or which one is most important, because there's been no one to show you what your business is worth on a year-by-year basis. And even more importantly, you haven't been shown how your business's price fluctuates in the mind of a buyer based on every little thing you do to it."

"Price fluctuation? You mean like a stock price?"

"Very similar, yes. Except it's not flashing red or green on the New York Stock Exchange, and the shares of your company are not traded daily among buyers and sellers. Fine-

Line's valuation is hidden both in the financial statements and outside them, but I promise you, sophisticated buyers know where to find it, and them knowing that puts you at a disadvantage."

"And you'll help me understand it?"

"That, and other things. You see, I want you to know their language, their strategies, frankly their games. If you know those, you'll have the best chance at winning at the closing. That's why I want to teach you to think like a buyer. What you do directly affects their perception of your business. You'll no longer be confused when buyers talk about multiples or value drivers. In fact, you may even turn the conversation around on them and ask for a purchase and sale agreement that throws their multiples and valuation approach out the window."

"I like the sound of that."

"I've seen it happen."

Dave understood. He realized he started talking with Bill Steele too soon and naively thought he could outmaneuver him. He hadn't anticipated Max Hatchet to come and tear his financial statements apart and talk about multiples. He had to admit he was thinking of himself and everything he had been able to get out of the company over the years, often instead of reinvesting in it. He had never thought to consider the thoughts of the one who was buying his business.

Everything that Bob Miagi said made sense, but there was one more question. "Tell me, then. If this team is going to help me sell my business, how do they work around my employees?"

"That's a good question, and it's a tricky one. Fortunately, there are ways around that. The first is access to your building. Some will need it. Others won't. Those that won't can make their contribution offsite and never come in contact with your employees. Some of those that do need to come on site and look at your files, layout, machinery, computers, etc. can do so after hours when no one is there."

"What about the process, HR, and sales consultants?"

"If we need them, yes, there will be people that have to come and observe business operations and improve them. In those instances, they will be on the premises during business hours and they will have contact with your employees. However, they will not mention anything about your intent to sell. And that's not their concern. If on the off chance they are asked why they're there, they will say they've been hired to help the company run better. It's a true statement, because that's exactly what we're trying to do. Remember, a smart buyer doesn't buy a company just so they can lay off people indiscriminately. They would prefer that employees, especially the key employees, remain in the company and continue contributing toward future growth. And it may even be the case where your buyer has a portfolio of other companies. Some of FineLine's employees can work in those subsidiaries and find advancement opportunities. You just never know who will be the buyer of a small business. Sometimes it's quite amazing."

"Makes sense," Dave said.

"I'll also coach you on how to work personally with your employees while preparing for a sale. You've never been through this before, but I can help guide you so you're not caught off guard."

"Okay. It all sounds good. So, how does our agreement work?"

Bob nodded, slid his black folder in front of him, and opened it. "Let me show you."

As Bob explained the contract agreement, Dave sipped his black coffee. It was lukewarm, but he was feeling better. A plan was forming in his head about how everything would work. For the first time, he could picture the strategy in his mind. It would take longer than he thought, perhaps years. But with the right team and the right strategy, he imagined that a better future was possible.

A CLOSER LOOK

Dave is learning how to form a strategy to set up his business for a premium sale. As the book Good to Great suggests, the first thing to do for any venture is to decide who gets on the bus. For a first-time business seller, this can be confusing because he's not sure who would be the right player for the job.

This is where expertise comes in handy. An experienced M&A Advisor will know which business professionals are necessary to help the business owner prepare for two specific exit phases. The first phase is the establishment of the business as an attractive purchase. The second is the close and the completion of the sale. Each of these phases requires many steps for a successful outcome. Since these events consist of a one-time circumstance that may or may not benefit the business seller, the business seller must gather as much experience as possible through the knowledge of an experienced team.

Once that team is together, the M&A Advisor will work with that team, establishing the game plan and launching its execution so the team will work together and help the business seller win.

DECISION

Dave left the coffee shop feeling excited. In a way, he was looking forward to getting back to business, but it wasn't just that. He wanted to win big, even if that took longer than he thought. He was going to get through his cancer, but he was also going to get to work. He looked forward to learning something new, how to exit his business like a champion.

Speaking of champions, Dave wondered how Mark Bragowski was doing. He hadn't talked with Mark since the day of Mark's closing. He thought it might be worth it to bounce Bob Miagi's strategy off of him since he just went through the selling experience. Rather than pick up the phone, Dave decided to drive by Mark's business, just in case, to say hello.

31
DAY 17 FRIDAY
9:10 A.M.

Dave walked into Mark Bragowski's reception area. Dave checked his appearance in a nearby mirror and was satisfied that he looked far better than the last time he was in Mark's building. Mark's door in the hallway was closed.

Terri was sitting at her desk. She looked up from her computer, startled. Her hair was slightly out of joint. Her face appeared stressed. Even her dress had some wrinkles, which was unlike her.

"Hi, Terri. Is Mark in?" Dave said.

Terri didn't smile. "Hold on." With no hesitation, she picked up the phone.

Through Mark's closed doors, his booming voice shouted like an angry cowboy, "I told you not to bother me!"

Terri didn't even wince. "Dave Garrity is here. He just heard you through the doors." Terri hung up the phone. "We'll see what he does."

Dave's eyes widened. Before Mark's business sale, everything was calm and peaceful. Today, the tension hung in the air like a fog. He had never heard Bragowski shout like that, even through closed doors. What was going on? Something happened, something bad.

Bragowski's office door swung open. Mark Bragowski walked into the hallway. He was wearing dress pants and a golf shirt, but his shirt was untucked in places over his belt. His eyes were red. His forehead was wrinkled. He put a fake smile on and walked up to Dave, extending his hand. "Hi, Dave. Glad you stopped by."

Dave shook his hand. "Hey, Mark."

"Come on in," Mark said. "Can Terri get you anything?"

Dave declined. Dave followed Mark into his office, where Mark shut the door. Mark's desk hadn't changed much, except for more stacks of papers. The wastebasket was full. The cabinet drawers were open, and files were exposed. The large fishing picture on the wall was off its kilter. "What can I do for you?" Mark said.

"I hadn't seen you since the closing. I was wondering how it went."

Mark leaned forward. A hint of pain flashed over his face. The man closed his eyes and opened them. Dave wondered if he detected tears watering under his eyelids. "It's done."

Dave waited. For a man who couldn't keep from bragging, Mark said little. "How'd it go?" Dave said.

Mark shook his head. "Not like I hoped."

"Did you sell?"

Mark took a deep breath. "Yeah. Unfortunately."

"Unfortunately?"

"Not like I thought I would."

Dave cocked his head. "What happened?"

"Damn buyers. They laid a trap for me, and I didn't even see it coming."

"What kind of trap?"

"I'd rather not say," Mark said. "I already said too much."

Dave nodded. "If it will make you feel any better, I just lost a deal for my business. A guy with a New York firm tried to lowball me. I also think it cost me a client since I was spending too much mental energy trying to manage my own deal. But I'm regrouping. I'm going to hire an M&A Advisor and build a team."

"Well, the Monday morning quarterback in me tells me that's what I should've done," Mark said.

Dave was shocked. In all the years of knowing Mark Bragowski, the man never admitted to a mistake. Never. "What do you mean?"

Mark looked up.

Yes, Dave thought, there were tears in his eyes.

Mark said, "Maybe I can warn you so what happened to me doesn't happen to you."

"Warn me?"

"You know, when a firm comes calling and makes an offer of so much money, you can't help but feel you struck oil. You go and tell your wife and your family. You make plans. You talk up your business in every sort of way. And all the while the buyers are nodding their heads, agreeing with you, letting your mouth run about how your company's potential is the next private rocket ship to take investors to the moon." Mark rubbed his forehead. "Of course, if that were true, I'd hang onto the saddle and cash out later for two or three times today's offer."

"What'd they do?"

"They told me to prove it," Mark said. "Me and my stupid mouth."

"Prove what?"

"Everything. As the closing got nearer, they came at me with questions. Wanted to evaluate the company's growth potential. I told them, 'Of course there's growth potential!' They didn't disagree. But in the days leading up to the closing, they changed the terms of the offer."

"Did they give you what you were asking for?" Dave said.

"Only on paper."

"How's that work?"

"In the conversations, they started talking more about what's called an 'earnout', meaning the way I'd get quite a bit of my asking price becomes contingent on future events."

"But, those events will happen, won't they?"

"Hell if I know."

"But you were so sure. . . "

"Half sure. Maybe less. I've got no idea. Hell, they got me talking up such a big game that I boxed myself in."

"Why didn't you walk away?"

"From the table? I don't know. Pride, mostly. Melissa was so excited for the deal to happen. I didn't want to pretend. I was a fool, I guess. I got a portion of what they initially offered. If I get the rest before I'm six feet under I'll be surprised."

"So you did get a check up front?"

"Yeah. But for far less than what I hoped."

"Well, that's good, isn't it, that you got paid something up front?"

Mark shook his head.

Dave said, "What are you going to do next? Racehorses and Italy?"

"Ha! No chance of that now. Melissa's very disappointed. Blames me for everything. I guess she's right. We haven't slept well since the closing." Mark shifted in his chair and bit his lip. "Not much I can do now. Just make sure we're covered through retirement, I suppose. With kids and grandkids getting into trouble these days, no telling what we'll need."

Dave leaned back. No wonder he hadn't heard from Mark.

A CLOSER LOOK

"The Hosin' at the Closin'." This is a term in the M&A world that exists because it happens. What Mark just described was one way that a closed deal ends in disappointment for the business owner. When the deal becomes contingent upon future events described by an overly enthusiastic seller, the buyer will often change the deal's terms so that a smaller amount of the initial offer is paid at the closing and the remainder is due upon the completion of certain future events. It's called an 'earnout' and an increasing number of deals have some form of earnout component.

The question is whether those future events that the earnout depends upon will happen.

Those future events are typically revenue and income goals. Of course, the business's chance of realizing those future events is much more uncertain because the enthusiastic seller won't be there to lead the company anymore, and he may have talked up a big game trying to increase the size of the offer. The seller has boxed himself in. Ignoring reality, the seller has agreed to a deal brought about by his own excitement.

When those future events don't materialize, the seller never gets his full payout. Worse, the seller knows the full payout is unlikely because he was overly optimistic about his company's prospects. Yet he goes through with the sale because he now has his reputation on the line, or his health is failing, or he's burned out. Was he fudging about his company's prospects, or was he completely telling the truth? The buyer's contingent deal is their way of saying, "Prove it," and putting the seller on the spot. Not willing to risk his reputation, the seller goes through with the sale and what he ultimately nets from the transaction is greatly reduced.

This is just one way there can be a "Hosin' at the Closin'." The buyer changes the terms because he perceives risk differently. Thus, as the closing approaches and time gets shorter, the buyer uses that pressure to change the terms. The seller becomes emotionally invested, believing he'll earn a windfall profit and retire. The buyer knows that the seller is more likely to go through with the sale, even if the terms change drastically in the buyer's favor.

The buyer is betting on the fact that, psychologically, it becomes difficult for the seller to walk away from the table, even if he's facing contingent terms.

The "Hosin' at the Closin'" is one of the reasons fifty percent of all business sellers are unsatisfied after they sell their business. It's not the only reason, but it's definitely up there. When the receiving price is far less than what was asked for, not only will the business seller have to deal with the challenge of finding purpose in retirement, but also he will have to adjust his expected lifestyle due to an unanticipated lower income level.

DECISION

Dave thanked Mark, said goodbye to Terri, and left the building. When he climbed into his truck, he sat for several moments. What had happened to Mark? It was like Lucy holding the football for Charlie Brown, and she yanked the ball away right as he was about to kick it. Had Mark's pride beaten him? Why did he go through with the sale? Why didn't he walk away? Was a business sale so psychological that sellers often fall into traps of their own making?

Dave shook his head. He realized that he, too, had been caught in a trap. All the talk about racehorses and international trips took his eye off the goal. What was his goal, anyway? At the end of the day, his goal was to live an identity and to be the best business owner he could be. He had dodged a bullet. If he had taken that offer, there was no telling what would have happened. No, he was better than that.

And he would be his best right up to the day he handed over the keys!

32
DAY 20 MONDAY
10:50 A.M.

After a weekend of coaching from Bob Miagi, Dave Garrity walked into FineLine Manufacturing like a new owner. He scheduled a manager's meeting for eleven a.m. He had prepared several documents, and he was excited to explain his company's new direction.

At ten-fifty a.m., Dave was waiting in the executive conference room. His documents were in a folder in front of him.

Diane appeared first. As she sat down, Cliff and Tim followed close behind. Nobody smiled except for Dave. Tim closed the door.

"Okay. I want to thank you all for coming this morning," Dave said. "I want to begin also by thanking you for your hard work over the years. I know things have been hectic. We have had some bad news with CWB, but I want you to know that I take the responsibility for it. In fact, looking back on everything, I realize there's a lot of things I could have done better."

"Dave," Diane said. "You've built this company."

"And I still am, except this time around I want to do it better. I want to do it with a team."

"We are a team," Tim said. "We do what we can to support you."

"And therein lies the problem. For a long time I've let my business be about me, about my being able to control things. But that's not good enough. The fact is I should be supporting you. You are all what makes FineLine Manufacturing great, not me."

"But, boss," Cliff said, "You're the salesman. Without you, we don't have any customers."

"Cliff, you're beating me to the punch. You're right. That is a problem. In fact, there are many problems I want to fix, but they all stem from me trying to control everything."

Dave pulled out his documents and slid them to Diane, Tim, and Cliff. The three of them promptly studied the papers. On the top page were a series of blocks arranged as steps, each one leading to a star that indicated the goal.

"First, I want you to know that the documents I'm handing to you are not set in stone. I want your input. This is a living document, which means I expect it to change at least quarterly (if not weekly) as we execute our plan."

"What are these steps?"

"That top page is our Strategic Plan. Those steps are the logical building blocks to achieve our goal."

"And our goal is. . . ?"

"What it says right there on the top. 'FineLine Manufacturing will be the number one quality gear manufacturer for production lines in the world.'"

Diane, Tim, and Cliff raised their eyebrows. "No offense, sir, but shouldn't we focus on surviving in the short term instead of planning for the long term?" Tim said.

Dave nodded. "I get it. What do we do about CWB? Look, we can only control what we can control. But no matter what, we can't let fear paralyze us. We will make adjustments in the short term, but we won't make adjustments that propel us into a worse position. We want to plan now for an objective that will make FineLine the best at what we do."

"But what about layoffs?" Cliff said. "Will I have to let anybody go on my team?"

"Who's to say? How will we know there will be any layoffs if we don't know where we're going?"

Cliff nodded. "Okay."

"If you'll turn the page, what you'll see is a situation. I tried my best to come up with our exact scenario as it exists today, listing a S.W.O.T. analysis."

"What is S.W.O.T. again?" Cliff said.

"Strengths. Weaknesses. Opportunities. Threats. But that's not all. I also took a shot at listing things we don't know, things we will want to consider and, as new information arrives, could cause us to change the course of our strategic plan."

"So, what are we trying to do?" Tim said.

"The first thing is to make sure we are all on the same page. I want all of you to review this document and add your input. Think it over the rest of the day and tonight, and we'll meet here the same time tomorrow morning."

"This seems pretty clear," Diane said.

"It'll be better with your input. And if I'm wrong anywhere, please don't hesitate to highlight it and let me know why you think I am."

"So, you are saying you're open to our suggestions?" Tim said.

"Yes," Dave said. He put his hands on the table and felt himself getting emotional. "When FineLine became a company, I prided myself on making the company about our people. Looking back, I could have done better at that. But I'm willing to change. I want you to know I value your input. Whatever we need to do, we'll discuss it in here and then execute it out there. One thing's for certain, whether we succeed or not, we're going to do it as a team. Together."

A CLOSER LOOK

When the owner shifts to a team-focused business-selling strategy, the next natural decision is probably to shift his leadership style. Rather than controlling everything on his own, he now must focus on creating a new company culture, one that sets direction, intent, measures, tasks, and boundaries for his employees to follow.

The shift in style will come with its challenges. As the business owner relieves himself of control, he has to learn to trust his new communication style. This can privately be nerve-wracking. He'll want to get his hands involved in all aspects of his business. But he must force himself to stay patient and not micro-manage.

If he gives a clear intent, his people, knowing their measures, tasks, and boundaries, will move forward in that direction. They will make mistakes, but the business owner needs to let them make those mistakes. In the process, the business owner will guide them so that they learn from those mistakes quickly. Eventually, the employees will learn the systems that work, and the organization as a whole will become far more knowledgeable about how to win than a single business owner can ever know on his own.

With a leadership style that encourages teamwork and clear communication, the company will set itself up for rapid action and achievement. Speed is necessary to help the business owner prepare his company for sale before life forces retirement too soon.

DECISION

Tim and Cliff left the conference room. As Dave was standing up, Diane held up her document in her hands and said, "You know, I like this. I have to tell you, though, the staff is nervous. Do you think it'll work?"

"I do. We may need some help in some areas, but whatever comes about, we're going to grow through this."

"I think it's exciting."

"Me, too," Dave said. "We may become something we never expected."

33
DAY 34 MONDAY
6:00 A.M.

Two weeks later, Dave sat in the coffee shop. His shoulder was healing nicely from the surgery, but it still pinched when he moved. Dr. Blackwood said the surgery had gone well. Dave's first radiation treatment was scheduled for later in the week, depending on how the surgery area healed. He was glad to get his treatment underway. The sooner he began, the sooner the episode would be behind him. By focusing on his business, he could get his mind off his health issues, at least for a little while.

Committing himself to the game plan, Dave had opted to meet with Bob Miagi on Monday mornings at six a.m. This way, he could get a jump on the business and head into work ready to go.

Bob entered the coffee shop, joined by two men. One was a tall man in a suit. The man had a winning smile. The other was a gruff-looking man with a stern face and a beard. His eyes portrayed seriousness. They approached Dave's table and sat down. Bob said, "Dave, I want you to meet Joe Morgan and Lee Krause. Joe's going to be our team's sales consultant, and Lee is our process consultant. They will both serve a role in helping us with our objectives."

Dave shook hands with Lee. "It's a pleasure to meet you."

"Likewise," Lee said.

"Lee and Joe will work together on some of FineLine's systems. Lee will be mostly involved in the operations.

"You've done this before, I take it?" Dave said.

"I've been in operations all my life. Began with a career in logistics, but that spawned into warehousing and systems management, including conveyor belts. I've been familiar with your gears for some time."

"From incoming supplies to manufacturing to finished product to shipping to quality control, if it gets made, Lee will know how to do it better," Bob said.

"Sounds good to me," Dave said.

Dave shook hands with Joe. "So you're the sales guy."

Joe chuckled. "You could say I've been around the block a few times, too."

"Joe's being modest," Bob said. "He's been in sales since right out of college. Managed teams both large and small, both locally and internationally. What's more, he's also had involvement in research and development."

Dave said, "You know, it's going to be hard for me to let go of selling our products and dealing directly with our customers. It's what I've always done."

Joe grinned. "It's usually that way. But what happens when you're not there?"

"Diane handles it."

"Is she in sales?"

"Well, sort of. She helps run the books and accounting. But somehow she took over customer service. She manages a few ladies who make calls to clients."

"But is she in sales?"

"You mean, like prospecting?"

Joe nodded.

Dave conceded. "No. She's not."

"So, you're looking to sell to a buyer, but when you exit you've got no one to handle sales."

"I guess I thought we'd hire someone during the transition period. You know, after the sale."

"Think like a buyer," Bob Miagi said. "Contingencies can reduce buyer confidence and kill a sale."

"So, you're saying I should have that in place before the sale. And I bet you're also going to say that that change, and many others, need to be in place and working for a while before any buyer believes in them."

"If you were buying a company, wouldn't you like to see a growing sales chart and know that systems are in place? And yes, all the other changes that we'll implement need to be working and dependable, and most of all, they need to survive without you being in your company after closing. It's as if we're rebuilding your business so that it works well no matter who owns it. Remember, this is what most sophisticated buyers want, an optimized business from day one of their ownership."

"I suppose so."

"How many customers do you have?" Joe said.

"About a hundred. Our largest customer now is Aerolift. But we've got several more that buy gears from us when a piece wears out. Because we focus so much on quality, our parts last a long time. And much of our sales, about 35%, is takeaway business, meaning we replace a competitor's product with ours."

"What's your failure rate?" Lee said.

"Failure rate?" Dave said.

"Correct. It's a number that can be used when your product or service fails to meet customer expectations, whether it's a defective product or a mistimed shipment."

"I don't think we keep that number. We do have issues from time to time, but it's not a data set we keep track of."

Lee didn't answer, but his eyes told Dave they'd soon delve into those numbers.

"Dave, Joe and Lee are going to look at your current processes. They are going to have to go into the office during business hours and see what's happening. Will you be comfortable with that?" Bob asked.

"If you want my honest answer, no. But I realize I'm going to have to trust you."

"I can understand what you're thinking," Joe said. "We're just here to make the company better, and adjust the systems, both sales and operations, so that they improve."

Dave said, "So, are you going to come in and help us with our sales scripts?"

"It will be a lot more than that," Joe said. "Right now, much of your business is coming from current customers, but the market is changing and you have a new competitor in your markets. What's their name again? Markdown Gears?"

"Yeah."

"A low-price competitor is trying to make your industry a commodity. If all you do is business as usual, you're going to be undercut as their quality catches up to yours."

"They make junk."

"Everybody makes junk until they get their systems working. Even Henry Ford thanked his initial Model-T buyers because that afforded him time to get the system right to make better cars. I'm telling you, if you stay where you are, if you don't optimize your sales processes, CWB won't be the only customer you lose."

"So what do you propose?"

"I want to do a deep dive into your customer base. We need a system that combines Sales, Marketing, and Research and Development. I'll bet there are products and services your current customers want, and will pay a premium for, but you aren't offering them."

"You mean make better gears? We're already the best in quality."

"There's always room for improvement," Lee said.

Joe added, "You're not thinking big enough. What about Operations consulting? What about shrink wrap and other products? What about automation? What about conveyor belt communications with customer service? What about flow charts and space management services?"

"I hadn't thought of those."

"These are just ideas. But Lee and I want to delve into your market to find ways to bring in more revenue. It's far more than just the scripts. We want to make sure you're not leaving any money on the table."

Dave tapped his pen on the desk. "Bob, how much are Joe and Lee going to cost?"

"I'll let them tell you that."

Joe and Lee pulled out their folders and slid Dave their documents. Joe said, "Here's my terms. You'll find there are three options. What I just mentioned is Option 2. There are other choices as well. It depends on the level of detail, and frankly success, that you're wanting."

"And here are mine," Lee said. "You'll see there is a plan and objectives that we'll work on together."

Dave flipped through the proposals and when he saw the cost his eyes widened. "Ouch."

"Does it hurt as bad as what you just went through with CWB?" Bob said.

Dave rubbed his forehead. "No."

"Dave, my job will be to streamline your operations so that your systems are clear and your employees can manage the business without you."

Joe said, "And my job, Dave, will be to find growing sales revenue streams and build systems around them. When those are in place, it will help your company's multiples and valuations increase tremendously."

"Meaning, when it's all said and done, I can sell for more than Mark Bragowski and I won't have to be there to oversee the shipping?"

"Yes, very likely."

"Okay. Let's do it!"

A CLOSER LOOK

The rubber meets the road in the execution, which can feel tough. When the process begins, the business seller will continue to face decisions that require change. Some of that change is personal. Some of that change is monetary, and it comes out of either his pocketbook or his company's. The thought of both can make him hesitate.

Each moment of hesitation, however, sets the sale back and makes the possibility of selling the company for less money more likely. The pressure of retirement grows with each passing day. At this point, the only way to attack it is action. The business owner must go forward with a team, dealing with all the nuances of newness and unfamiliarity. This will affect his nerves as he learns the nuances of new processes. It's not easy. But it is to be expected.

When this process begins, it can seem exciting. Later, though, within the first few weeks of the team getting to work, there will be friction. Sometimes that friction will come from the employees. Other times it will come from the exit team itself. Either way, change is necessary. If done the right way, there will be moments of light. During these moments, the business seller suddenly "gets it" and regains his nerves. His new approach to leadership may inspire him even more as he sees the growth and maturity of his employees.

DECISION

Dave agreed with Bob that Joe should come into the office this week. Joe planned to meet with Tim, Dave's Operations Manager, and Diane who oversaw Customer Service. He was also going to do some market research using familiar tools. Joe explained how he wanted to get a detailed understanding of FineLine Manufacturing's customers and look for any hints that suggested potential sales opportunities.

After the meeting was over, Dave shook hands with the two of them. It has been two weeks now since he made his decision to create an exit team. He was nervous but told himself he was doing the right thing.

Even if he no longer felt in total control.

34
DAY 62 MONDAY
9:15 A.M.

Five weeks later, Dave was feeling tired, but good. His radiation treatments were underway, and Dr. Blackwood seemed positive. Things were tougher at FineLine Manufacturing. Revenues had fallen compared to forecasts, and Dave had to make some decisions. Fortunately, his remaining customers had stayed on board. Aerolift was now FineLine Manufacturing's largest customer, and they placed a surprise one-time order that doubled revenues from Aerolift for the quarter. "Thank God for a little luck," Dave told his staff.

Dave met regularly with his new outsourced CFO, Roger Track, and his CPA, Frank Addington. Bob Miagi also introduced Dave to a business transaction attorney, Ken Bergman. On some occasions, the five of them met at the coffee shop. On others, it was online. As the meetings continued, Dave felt more and more confident in the choices he made. He was stretching his skills, but he liked where things were going.

Dave had brought Joe Morgan into the office to examine FineLine Manufacturing's sales processes. Dave and Joe met with Tim and Diane separately, and Joe stood with Dave as they watched the manufacturing and shipping operations.

They also observed Diane's customer service. When Joe first appeared, there were several nervous looks, but the consultant dutifully mentioned that he was "there to make the company better." When asked what that meant, he inquired of them about potential new products and ideas they may have gathered in their time servicing customers.

The staff was beaming with pride when they suggested twenty new product and service ideas. Each idea contained a series of reasons why they should work. Any suspicion about Joe's presence was suddenly changed into an opportunity to provide input. Joe promised them that he would evaluate their ideas. That, coupled with his market research, would be presented to Dave and the managers for their consideration. Dave was impressed with how Joe was approaching his business. Maybe it will be money well-spent after all, he thought.

With the employees feeling accountable, their morale improved. Dave was feeling that, at any moment, something good would happen. That's why he was so surprised when, as he sat at his desk looking at his updated Strategic Plan, Tim knocked on the door. "Can I come see you?" Tim said.

Dave waved him in. "Yes. I have some ideas for our new plan and I want to get your thoughts."

Tim shut the door and sat down. "Sir, I'm sorry to tell you this, but I've accepted a position with another company."

"What?" Dave said.

Tim slid a piece of paper across the desk. "This is my official resignation. I'm willing to give two-week's notice, if you'll accept it."

"Why?"

"Nothing against you, Dave. You've been great. But I see the numbers. We're not where we used to be when we had CWB, and I don't know how long things can be sustained here."

With things in turmoil, the last thing Dave wanted was to lose his operations manager. What would that do to morale? How would Mr. Miagi handle this? Though HR would disapprove, Dave imagined giving Tim a karate chop across the face. "But don't you see the changes we're making? Something good's going to happen soon. I can feel it."

"If Aerolift hadn't decided to revamp their conveyor belt system, we'd be hurting right now, big time."

"But they did, and we're surviving."

"I'm done with surviving. I've got a family to feed and the uncertainty that exists around here now threatens our security. As much as I appreciate you, it's time for me to move on."

"Where are you going?"

"I'd rather not say."

"It's Markdown Gears, isn't it?"

"I'd rather not say."

"You son of a b—-!"

"So, you're not going to take my two weeks–."

"Get out!"

Dave later called Bob Miagi. Miagi agreed that Dave did the right thing. A person with that much access to information didn't need to be working too closely with FineLine's proprietary process and intellectual property, especially with an exit strategy underway, and especially if the individual was leaving to work for a competitor.

When Tim left the office, Dave looked again at his Strategic Plan. Then he pulled out his list of current employees. Crossing Tim off the list, he examined the other names. "You know," he said to himself. "What we're building will only give someone else a great opportunity. There's bound to be changes. We're not going to fear change; we're going to embrace it!"

A CLOSER LOOK

Not everyone will appreciate a new leadership style, and often those who become most accountable will sift themselves out of the organization as things grow serious. Personnel challenges seem debilitating, and they usually are unless there is a strong communication strategy that emphasizes the Plan.

A proper communication strategy can more easily replace a loss in personnel. Hopefully, a lower-level employee will show eagerness to rise to the challenge. If the employee lacks the necessary skills, however, the business owner can seek outside help. He can then integrate new employees into the operations and the culture.

The important thing is that the business is becoming less dependent on any one person, the owner in particular. Instead, the business is an organization of its own, supplying mutual support to everyone who remains committed to its cause.

Every business will face challenges as it strives for growth. But just because those challenges appear doesn't mean all is lost. If handled correctly, it could be the change needed to propel the business to the next level.

DECISION

The news of Tim's departure shocked many of the FineLine Manufacturing employees. Most were quiet, and Dave saw the expressions on their faces as they wondered why he left. Was it because he knew something bad was coming? Should they be considering their options as well?

If Dave would keep the team together, now was the moment.

Dave stopped operations and called his employees together, holding his Strategic Plan. "Everyone," he said. "You have seen how we're making changes. We're working together, talking, and figuring things out. I want you to know I am committed to you and accountable to each of you. With our changes, you all have had more freedom to add your input, but with that freedom comes accountability. It's up to you to see it through. I'll give you everything I can to help you succeed. But it's a fight right now. I get it. Not everyone can handle our new accountability, and not everyone can embrace the direction we're headed. I get that, too. But with each change comes opportunity. I feel something good is going to happen soon. It may be right around the corner. Perhaps you feel it, too. Our plan doesn't change in the absence of any one person. It changes if the team says it changes. All of us make this thing work."

When he was finished, Dave scheduled a manager's meeting for the next day so they could examine their plan and decide on any changes.

35
DAY 63 TUESDAY
8:58 A.M.

Dave sat in the executive conference room. It was two minutes until nine. Diane and Cliff walked inside and sat down. The room felt emptier with Tim gone. Dave would have to fill his position. Who would it be? Diane? She was always personal, cared, and knew the numbers. She was always on top of her game. Cliff, on the other hand, was closer to manufacturing. He knew the gears, the operations, and the delivery to their customers. If he promoted either of them, who underneath them would fill their shoes? Or, would he look outside the company? Was there a candidate who would be perfect for the job? Then again, what was the job? What did the Strategic Plan say? Did we need Tim's role? Would his departure save the company money?

"Dave, how's the treatment going?" Diane said.

"Good. Shoulder's got a scar on it, and radiation is about done. Doc feels positive about where we're at."

"How many more treatments do you have?"

"One more next week. Kathy and I are just praying everything's gone."

"Feels a little empty in here," Cliff said.

Dave nodded. "I don't disagree. But let me ask you, how do you like the changes so far?"

Diane said, "The front office feels good. Like a weight has been lifted and they can do more to help our customers."

"Good," Dave said.

"In the back, we're a little tired working on some of the new product ideas, but I have to say the team is enjoying coming up with new solutions. It's been better than shipping the same gears over and over again."

"So you like Joe's ideas?"

Diane and Cliff both said, "Yeah."

"You know, most of them were really your ideas – well, yours and the staff's."

"He had a way of helping us bring them to life, though," Diane said.

"And communication is better," Cliff said. "I've been talking with the front office more in the last few weeks than I had in all the years I've been here. That's a good thing."

"That's good to know," Dave said. "Let me ask you, what happened to Tim?"

Diane shrugged. "Can't really say. He never gave me any indication."

"Same here," Cliff said. "But, he was quieter, more reserved the last few weeks."

"Do you think he was helping?"

"At a minimum."

"What did he do that directly helped you?"

"He handled the ordering. Made sure I had my supplies."

"Can you handle that?"

Cliff's eyes widened. "I've never done that. What should I do?"

Dave remembered his training from Bob Miagi and referenced the Strategic Plan. "You see our intent. While our long term goal is to be the best in the industry at what we do, right now we're fine-tuning our operations to streamline our processes."

"How do you want me to do that?"

"Well, I'll work with you to handle our ordering processes, what we need and when. But you'll be closer to the situation than I will. If there are any changes you'd recommend, would you be willing to look into them?"

"You'll let me do that, Dave?"

"You'll still be accountable for the results. I want to use the best quality in our products, but there may be new designs we haven't thought of."

"We've got ideas," Cliff said enthusiastically.

"Great. Make sure the shipments get out in time each day. But spend ten percent of each day, or whatever time you have left, brainstorming new ideas."

Cliff swelled up with pride. "Yes, sir!"

A CLOSER LOOK

As things get chaotic, it will be tempting for the business seller to want to control new or changing processes. He can't do that, however, if he wants his company to expand, if he wants his people to flourish. The fact is that no person in a top-level office of a lower middle-market company like

FineLine can know everything that goes on at every lower level. What he must learn to do is trust his people to solve problems. The owner can give directions, but he must resist jumping in front of his employees and doing their job for them. He can help and do some of it with them, but only if they ask for or appear to need help. He should not do the job for them. Instead, he should let them make the effort and learn. Once it's over, the business owner and the employee should work together and write down the checklist of tactics needed to do the job better next time.

Ultimately, optimization becomes a series of discoveries and testing. It's the scientific method, except it's used for efficiency and effectiveness. The business owner is learning what makes his business compete in the current market and discovering new ways to serve his stakeholders, including customers, employees, investors, and suppliers.

Finally, it's important to document these discoveries in checklists. These discoveries transform into instructions for the company operations manual. They become procedures that can be followed for optimum effectiveness. Having these checklists instills accountability and confidence in the team. It improves morale, too, as the employees give input into their discoveries. The documented processes inside the manual will optimize the company. This manual will help comfort the buyer as he considers the company's value in terms of price.

By letting go and becoming a leader, the business owner sees the changes advancing the company rapidly. It's when these things all come together that the magic happens.

DECISION

Dave sat with Cliff and went over Tim's supply ordering book. As they went through it, they noticed several decisions Tim had made that they could improve. Dave was tempted to write down a checklist and give it to Cliff for him to execute, but he leaned back. Miagi had reminded Dave to let the staff work on their own checklists. So, Dave suggested that Cliff create a checklist to support the company's manufacturing efficiency and effectiveness. Cliff agreed. Dave asked Cliff how he planned to get it done. Cliff explained how he would examine the product and come up with an ordering schedule based on supplies. Dave finally asked Cliff if he needed anything before he got started. "Just confirm the budget for me," Cliff said. Dave promised to get that from Diane and bring it to him in an hour. Then he left the warehouse and returned to his office.

As he sat in his office chair behind his desk, Dave felt nervous. Letting go was hard for him. But he had to trust his direction. He had asked Cliff three vital questions. Did he understand what needed to be done? How did he plan to do it? Did Cliff need anything from Dave? Cliff had answered all three questions, and now Dave had to take him at his word.

Dave picked up the phone and called Diane.

"Yes, Dave?"

"Can you pull up the ordering budget and print a copy? I need to walk it over to Cliff. Before I do, I want to get your opinion about it."

"I'll have it on your desk in five."
"Great. See you in a few."

36
DAY 90 MONDAY
10:40 A.M.

Four weeks after Tim's departure, FineLine Manufacturing's employees were moving about their business in a new way. Dave noticed there was more emotion. Both laughter and celebration filled the halls and the warehouse.

But they needed a win, a real win with a new customer.

Joe Morgan's research presented a new opportunity. It seemed there appeared to be a problem in Aerolift's supply chain, caused by a gear that slowed production. Upon further examination, the slowdown wasn't a fault of FineLine's gears, but a design inefficiency within Aerolift's manufacturing process. Dave and his team looked into the problem. They emailed customer surveys to their client list, and the results astounded them. They found that the same problem was happening with their other customers.

"Why hadn't we found this before?" Cliff said. "It was always there, staring us in the face!"

"Let's not worry about the past," Dave said. "Let's find a solution to their problem and find out how much they'll pay us to fix it."

The team, with Joe's input, created a new gear design, one that solved the manufacturing slowdown and added greater efficiency within their customer's manufacturing processes, with the potential to save them millions of dollars. Next, Lee Krause worked with the team to implement new gear manufacturing guidelines and quality control. It was a great chance for Dave to see the consultants in action. He appreciated how they worked with his employees, discussing all strategies in a coordinated effort.

When the design and the production systems were finished, Dave leaned back and congratulated his team.

Joe leaned forward, however, and said, "You're not done yet."

"What do you mean?" Dave said.

"This whole process you just went through, it's an opportunity. Create a video of the process. Show how FineLine discovered the problem, worked on a new gear design, and solved the customer's problem. Put it out there in marketing material online and on your website. It will differentiate you from the low-cost competition and show that you're innovative and emphasizing your customer's success, not your own."

"He's exactly right," Lee said.

"But what if our competitor sees our operations and tries to copy it?"

"It's better to be the one copied than the one doing the copying. If your customers see that you're ahead of everyone else in innovation, that will keep you first in their minds."

Dave smiled and looked at his employees. "Diane, Cliff. Are you ready to get in front of a camera?"

"I'd better comb my hair," Cliff said.

The team laughed and then exited the conference room.

In an after-hours meeting, Dave met with Bob, Lee, and Joe. They wrote a script for the video and analyzed all its components. After several drafts, they agreed on the script. Dave would show it to Diane and Cliff the next day and ask for their input, being sure to make any adjustments as they felt necessary.

When the script was ready, Dave invited Katelyn, his daughter, to use her creativity and design expertise to produce a video. Dave had always been impressed with his son's financial success, but he was proud of Katelyn's creative capacity. She directed the employees and staff before the camera like a true professional, instructing them to say their lines, use proper emotion, and get the lighting right. Then she took the recordings, put them into video-editing software, added music, text, and animation components, and then created a .mp4.

"This is great!" Dave said. "What do we do with it?"

"Two things," Katelyn said. "Keep the large format on your YouTube channel, while breaking it down into small-form content to be used for your Facebook, TikTok, Twitter, and Linked-In accounts."

"She's right," Joe said.

Bob nodded. "No time like the present to do what she's saying."

Dave grinned at his daughter. "How do you know all this?"

"I learned from you, Dad. Always keep a few tricks up your sleeve."

Dave hugged her, feeling more proud than he had in years.

A CLOSER LOOK

Contrary to popular belief, optimism comes before accomplishment. It always does. When a business seller shifts his exit strategy to a team-oriented approach, a newfound optimism will permeate the organization. Yes, those not on board will sift themselves out, but those who remain will find a sense of belief different from the way things were. Why does this happen? The answer is simple. When the business seller runs his business correctly, everything about the company feels different. Discoveries create new efficiencies. New efficiencies create new opportunities. New opportunities create more discoveries. And the circle continues.

More importantly, the people see it happen. They become accountable for their processes and they gain an understanding of how their efforts contribute to a cause greater than themselves. It feels good to matter. Everyone in the company strives for that feeling.

When a team gets rolling, it's hard to stop. Others outside the company, including vendors and consultants, suddenly want to come help. The enthusiasm becomes contagious. The more people contribute, the cycle spins faster, compounding successes with each passing moment. Then, one day, a shift happens. Gamers would call it a "Level Up." Athletes call it "being in the zone". The business, now operating efficiently, suddenly acquires a new opportunity. It's the reward for a coordinated team effort, attracting growth and resources they can use to advance to the next level.

DECISION

A few days after releasing the marketing videos, Dave was sitting in his office. The Strategic Plan was underway. There had been some changes to the original plan, but they made fewer changes the more they learned. Now, the direction appeared solid. Everyone was on board. The employees were communicating with each other and working together. The phone rang. Ava's voice came through the speaker. "There's a call for you, Dave."

"Is it a Solicitor?"

"I don't think so."

"Ok. I'll pick it up." Dave shook his head. "Let it be a win," he said. Then he pressed the button and picked up the receiver. "Dave here."

"Hello, Mr. Garrity?"

"Yes."

"This is Bill Ontko. I'm the purchasing director at Apex Engineering Solutions. My supply chain manager saw one of your videos online about how you solved the conveyor belt issue at critical junctions. We're in need of a more reliable supplier, and wondered if we could discuss doing business with you."

"Certainly, Mr. Ontko. What exactly are you looking for?"

"We need eighteen three-fifths gears that will hold an angular momentum of 900 nanometers at those junctures."

"That's quite a load capacity."

"We're supplying a defense contractor, so you can imagine."

"Understood."

"Is that something you can handle?"

"Absolutely. When do you need them?"

"As soon as you can get them to us."

"We're on it. Will that be all?"

"Hold on a sec. . ." Mr. Ontko's voice became somewhat muffled as he conversed with another person in the room. Dave strained to hear but wasn't sure what the other party was saying. The tone, though, sounded positive. "Okay. Yes. We typically have breakage in our gears on average nine per week. Could you resupply those on a regular basis?"

"We could, but I'm curious whose gears you're using. Ours have been tested and have a long lifespan."

"Our gears run in extreme conditions."

"Then you're looking at 5,000 hours, at least."

"That's pretty good."

"It's what we do."

"If it's alright, we'd like to come and see your operations."

"Gladly. Shall I get my travel agent to help?"

"No. I'll have my receptionist set it up. I'll also be bringing Elliot Harris, our CEO. He will be interested in your operations, too."

"Terrific. When can we be expecting you?"

"We'll be there Wednesday."

"See you then." Dave and Bill said their goodbyes, and Dave hung up the phone. A defense contractor would be a huge win for FineLine Manufacturing. Depending on who it was, it could be bigger than CWB. Much, much bigger.

Dave leaned back, stretched his arms above his head, and felt the relief come through his fingertips.

37
DAY 174 MONDAY
2:35 P.M.

Three months later in Frank Addington's CPA office, Dave met with his All-Star team. They couldn't meet at FineLine Manufacturing because servicing several new customers, including Apex Engineering Solutions, required expanding manufacturing operations during night hours. New shifts had to be hired just to keep up with the work. Bob brought in an HR consultant to help Dave create his Organizational Charts. This would assist his team with communications and accountabilities. Lee Krause's operational processes helped get the new employees acclimated to their jobs, and the ramp-up period was greatly reduced. There was now a sales manager and a sales team whose job was to establish relationships with customers. Even with the new personnel, the revenue growth far outpaced expenses.

"Your ratios are looking good," Roger Track said. As the Outsourced CFO, a man with heavy supply chain manufacturing experience, he had been instrumental in helping Dave and Frank, Dave's CPA, learn the nuances of exit planning finances for FineLine's business. At first, Frank had been a little quiet when Roger came on board, but these days the two worked well together, sometimes communicating in financial and tax lingo so quickly it sounded to Dave like another language.

"Yes, they are," Frank said. "The balance sheet is showing tremendous ratios. Not only that, the income and cash flow statements look amazing. We've only got a few quarters of reporting to go on, but if you look at them month over month the numbers are parabolic."

"And the multiples are trending in the right direction." Bob Miagi said. "If this keeps up, FineLine could be a 2x or 3x company not long from now. Roger, what are your thoughts?"

Roger lifted his reading glasses and held the papers in his hands. "Because we have yet to show consistency, I'm a little limited in what I would suggest. But, at a minimum I'd say we're on track to ask for a valuation of fifteen."

"Fifteen what?" Dave said.

"$15 million," Roger answered. "And that's a safe bet. If we show consistency."

Dave opened his mouth. "Really?"

"It's what the numbers are telling us."

"I can't believe this is working," Dave said. "I mean, I had hoped for something positive. I just didn't think it would happen so fast. And for so much."

"It doesn't always go so well," Bob said. "Sometimes our clients struggle to make the changes we suggest. But you were terrific. You made a complete change in how you were running your business, and the buyer pool will recognize it."

Dave leaned back in his chair. He had been through so much. Cancer. Business stress. Home stress. Uncertainty. But here he was, sitting before financial experts who were telling him his company had a valuation much higher than even he expected. "You know, I have a friend who sold his business several months ago," Dave said. "He didn't do anything you guys did. Thought he could do it on his own. After the sale, I found out that the buyer changed his terms on him at the last minute. He went through with it anyway. Today, he's back to work, doing consulting. Before the sale, he had plans of travel and racehorses. As far as I know he has yet to get on a plane to Europe or ride a horse."

"It happens," Ken Bergman, the business transaction attorney, said. "More often than needs to."

"I'm just so thankful for what you all have done for me."

"Don't thank us yet," Bob said. "There's one more thing to discuss."

"What's that?"

"Optimization wasn't the only part of our contract. The next phase is the sale. When the company is positioned within certain levels, it's my job to research and contact potential buyers."

Dave held his breath. "What are you saying?"

"Per the terms of our agreement, I found one, a potential buyer for FineLine. Their name is Integrity Industries. They're a family office-backed company based out of Texas."

"I haven't heard of them."

"They aren't much for promoting themselves. They like to buy industries with a focus on building up companies for the long haul. They form strategic partnerships within their subsidiaries to leverage price opportunities so that they can gain strength against the competition."

"So they aren't going to come in and fire all my employees?"

"They're not like that. They like companies with similar cultures to theirs. It makes the transition smooth. Their approach is simple: if the company is running well, they want to make it run even better."

"What about the valuation?"

"We still have to discuss an NDA, but based on my preliminary conversation with them, they're open to starting the conversation at twelve."

"$12 million?"

"Yes."

"They won't try to hose me at the closing, will they?"

Ken Bergman leaned forward. "I'll make sure they won't. Every communication will go through my firm and Bob. At the first sign of anything, we'll be right on top of it."

"Thanks," Dave said.

"But I will tell you this," Ken said. "When a buyer knows the seller has a team like us, it's rare they try anything funny. A seller that hires a team for optimization is a quality seller who is working to sell a quality company. No doubt they'll do their research, but without any red flags, they get excited real quick."

"Okay. So what's the next step?"

"Pack your bags, Dave. You and I are going to Texas."

A CLOSER LOOK

As the company's optimization is reflected in the tax returns and financial statements, the company becomes a quantifiable prospect for potential buyers. The M&A Advisor, having assisted the seller with putting together a team, has now done a lot of the work to get the company ready for sale.

This then becomes the moment where the rubber meets the road. With attractive financial and tax statements, the seller and his team now have a company they can put up for sale. Not only can an optimized company attract the right buyer, but it can also attract multiple buyers, thereby creating a market for the company and raising its valuation and price. It may even be possible to make two or more buyers compete for the opportunity to buy. The competitive bid process goes by several different names, and it's a lot more work for the M&A Advisor, but the goal is to squeeze out a 10-20% higher price to be paid by the buyer. Very few for-sale companies are successful in making buyers compete. But when they do compete, the seller wins.

It's important to note that this moment, the moment when the seller realizes it's time to let his company fly on its own, is often an emotional one. On the one hand, he's extremely happy with the prospects for his sale. Not only has his company grown, but he has as well. He is about to achieve the highest honor a business owner can have: being one of the 2% of business owners who successfully sell their business and are happy once they have.

But what does happiness mean? Having worked so hard for so many years, the business seller will undoubtedly have questions about the remainder of his life. But there will be time for that shortly. The M&A Advisor, tasked with finding a buyer, will use his resources to research and inquire as to a potential buyer's interest. It will be his job to look for the right buyer who appreciates the company and its potential and its culture. More importantly, it will be his job to represent the seller's best interest and to bring a quality buyer to the table who won't hurt his client.

At this point, the business seller is very close to winning the game. A few more steps with his team and he'll cross the endzone for the touchdown and celebrate with his team after the win.

DECISION

Dave sat on his bed at home and slipped off his shirt. The scar from his cancer surgery was on his back. He put on a nightshirt and leaned back.

"I'm so sorry you have that scar," Kathy said. She was sitting up in bed, a book about thoroughbreds on her lap.

"Well, I'm just glad I'm still alive that you can comment on it," Dave said. Bernie walked up to Dave's bedside and panted with his large furry smile, his tongue hanging from his mouth. "Good boy. Go lie down," Dave said. Bernie obeyed and went to the center of the floor, circled three times, and lay down.

"Are you all packed?" Kathy said.

"Yes. Plane leaves at eight. I need to get up early to make sure I get there."

"Are you sure you don't want me to come with you?"

"No. The team will handle it. Bob has everything covered. We should be back in two days."

"Okay," Kathy said. "You know, I do have a thought."

Dave rolled over. "What?"

"If we do get a thoroughbred, I thought of a name."

"What's that?"

"FineLine for the Win."

Dave chuckled. "I like that," he said. He leaned up to Kathy and kissed her on the mouth. Then he turned out his bedside light, closed his eyes, and fell asleep.

38
DAY 258 MONDAY
SUNSET

"Honey, could you please pour some more wine?" Kathy said.

Dave picked up the bottle and gently poured the red merlot into her glass. "I can't believe wine is cheaper than Coca Cola here in Italy."

"This is a great trip," Kathy said. She inhaled the Tuscan air while they sat on chairs overlooking the Italian sunset from their villa's balcony. After Dave had finished pouring, he set the bottle down, leaned back, and let his muscles relax.

"What's next for us?" Kathy said.

"I'm trying to figure that out," Dave said.

"Are you going to do some consulting?"

"Like Mark?" Dave laughed. "Not like he's doing it, no. If I were to help someone, I think I'd volunteer my time."

"Is that what you're going to do?"

"Actually, I've been thinking of doing more charity. I want to help our church, and maybe the local art museums. My alma mater is always looking for help. Maybe I'll do something with them."

"We have another trip to Connecticut coming up."

"We just went there," Dave said. "We don't want to smother them."

Kathy tilted her head. "Don't keep me from my grandbabies."

Dave laughed and gently reached for Kathy's hand. "Only until we get back from Italy."

Kathy sipped her wine. "Okay."

"You know, looking back at this whole thing, we really lucked out."

"Well, you did it, honey."

"No. I screwed up. The team did it. Bob organized the team. He trained me. And he found Integrity Industries who was overjoyed at the chance to buy FineLine. If it wasn't for Bob Miagi and the rest of the team, no telling what would have happened to us."

"I shouldn't have put all that pressure on you," Kathy said.

"I put a lot of it on myself," Dave said. "That and the cancer. If I hadn't been so doggone stubborn I'd have avoided all that stress in the first place."

"You didn't know."

"True. But not knowing can get you ruined. I wish there was a resource out there to help business owners know what to expect before they try to do it all on their own."

"Isn't that what Bob does?"

"It is. But maybe I can help. Maybe there should be a book out there. You know, something to let business owners know that selling a business is different than selling a product or service, or selling a piece of real estate."

"Why don't you write the book?"

Dave leaned back and sipped some of his wine. "You know, maybe I will. Maybe I just will."

A CLOSER LOOK

Once a sale is completed, the business owner can do nothing else than process the feelings of his situation. Is he happy? Scared? Relieved? Stressed? Much of this depends on the outcome of his sale compared to his expectations. If the outcome met or surpassed his expectations, he'll likely be happy and relieved. If the outcome does not meet his expectations, he'll feel stressed or, worse, scared and he'll have to go through the five stages of grief all over again.

The happy seller will have more options than the unhappy one. Not only will the unhappy one have to deal with the loss of anticipated dreams, but he'll also be faced with living the reality of life with a lower income. This will affect decisions and he'll have fewer options through the remainder of his life. He could even be forced to work again in some capacity whereby he'll add to his income for a time until health prevents him from doing so.

The happy seller, on the other hand, will have different decisions. He could return to work and earn an income, but is that his purpose? What about family and children and grandchildren? What about politics and the country in which he lives? What about charities and foundations to help future generations? What about the church and eternal questions? The happy seller will have time and resources to explore these questions, but he'll also want to come up with the answers and get moving. The average lifespan of a male after retirement is 11-13 years. Again, this is average. The financial world has an unspoken concern for retirees who stop working and don't find something else to do. These men see health issues and death much sooner than the average male, even if their retirement is successful.

Thus, while the unhappy seller may be forced to choose a new goal upon selling his business, the happy one will want to choose one quickly and find a way to continue giving to the world. He'll have more options to give his time and experience, but he should spend his time doing those options, getting a feel for them, and contributing to the world in his newfound capacity.

Of course, all this comes right after the initial celebration. Once he takes the time to celebrate with his family, he will want to get back onto a schedule. It's been said everyone needs someone to love, something to do, something to hope for, and something to believe in. Retirement does not end these needs. If he finds the answers to these, his life and legacy will continue well into retirement and beyond through the relationships he builds along the way.

DECISION

While the sun was setting in the west, and Kathy leaned back in her chair, Dave's phone buzzed.

"Who is it?" Kathy said.

"Text message," Dave said. He picked up his cell phone. "Wouldn't you know it?"

"What?" Kathy said.

Dave raised his wine glass to make a toast. "We have another member of the family?"

"We do?"

"The foal dropped early. Congrats, Honey. We own a thoroughbred." He sipped his wine in celebration.

"Oh. I wanted to be there."

Dave set his glass down and said, "I promise we'll go see him as soon as we get back."

"Are you happy with the name?"

"I've been meaning to tell you. I think I want to change it."

"You do? To what?"

"Exit Teams for the Win."

While Kathy pondered the new name, the sun set beyond the western foothills, casting shadows over the cool countryside. Dave leaned back, looked up, and thanked God.

"Exit Teams for the Win? Hmmm. It has a nice ring to it," Kathy said.

"It does," Dave said. "It sure does."

39
CONCLUSION

Thank you for reading Exit Teams. I hope the experience gave you several things to think about as you grow your business and prepare to sell it. This story was designed to help you understand the concepts necessary for a successful business exit. By now you probably realize you're always preparing your business for a sale. You'll exit your business, either on your terms or not. You can have your plan or you can have someone else's plan. You must make critical choices about how you will proceed and who you will enlist to your aid. They are not easy choices, but the earlier you begin thinking of them, the easier they are.

A quick disclaimer here. I must mention that many variables must align perfectly for a business to achieve a 3x growth valuation in the time it took for Dave to achieve his objective. While a two-hour movie often shortens a storyline for dramatic effect, this story about Dave did likewise, and Dave's example, while it does happen, is more the exception than the rule. Sometimes it takes years for a business owner in Dave's situation to fix his business.

I designed this book in a story format to help you understand the experiences and challenges of a business sale, not to give you an expectation. My intent was for you to understand many of the emotions a business owner may face before an exit, and I in no way promise similar results in a similar time and fashion as this story relates since no two situations are the same.

After you read Exit Teams, I would ask a favor of you. Please take some action to spread the word. Tell a friend about this book. Write a review on Amazon. You can also contact me directly for speaking engagements or, if you're so inclined, a personal consultation for your specific situation.

I can be reached using the contact information below.

Bob Tankesley
770-633-1083
Bob@ExitTeams.com
www.exitteams.com

40
TRAINING CAMP

[Join Training Camp]

Want More Exit Strategy Insights?

Click the Button above to watch a **free 40-minute video training** with Bob Tankesley, author of Exit Teams.
Inside, you'll learn:
- What your business is really worth
- How to think like a buyer
- Why only 4% of businesses sell—and how to be one of them

Whether you're planning your exit now or later, this video gives you clarity, confidence, and a smarter strategy.

Press the Button above or click on https://bit.ly/ExitTeams to start watching.

41
A CLOSER LOOK INDEX

1. Selling suddenly becomes a thought. (Chapter 2)

2. The idea of selling can cause stress. (Chapter 3)

3. Older business owners get tired with age, which can cause business systems to slip. (Chapter 4)

4. Sharing the idea of selling a business with family also creates stress. (Chapter 5)

5. Deciding to sell comes down to two reasons: Personal or Business. (Chapter 6)

6. Typically a business owner approaches an inside buyer first. (Chapter 7)

7. Family reactions to the idea of a business sale vary across the emotional spectrum. (Chapter 8)

8. Pressure grows upon the business owner as he explores selling while still managing the business. (Chapter 9)

9. Naivety about selling often leads to early mistakes.

(Chapter 10)

10. While How to Sell Your Business books assume a business is sellable, the numbers tell a different story. (Chapter 11)

11. Employee Stock Ownership Plans (ESOPs) are often explored early in the selling process. (Chapter 12)

12. While it's natural to seek counsel from business owners who have completed a sale, there are some risks. (Chapter 13)

13. ESOPs make sense in a narrow range of business conditions. Pluses and Minuses. (Chapter 14)

14. Health is a major factor when considering selling. (Chapter 15)

15. Dreams of a windfall can add more stress to the business owner. (Chapter 16)

16. Concentration Risk can make a business unsellable. (Chapter 17)

17. Evaluate the advice of an accountant as you would any other professional. (Chapter 18)

18. Business Buyers know the psychological game and play into the seller's ego to drive the price down. (Chapter 19)

19. Emotional reactions vary after receiving a low-ball offer. (Chapter 20)

20. The business owner's options after receiving a low-ball offer. (Chapter 21)

21. There are generally two types of service providers who assist business sellers: listing agents/business brokers and Mergers and Acquisitions (M&A) Advisors. (Chapter 22)

22. Seminars on selling a business. (Chapter 23)

23. At some point, employees will learn of a business sale. (Chapter 24)

24. Receiving an offer isn't the end of the game. (Chapter 25)

25. The stress of selling can cause family breakdowns. (Chapter 26)

26. Many business-selling stress points can converge into a crisis. (Chapter 27)

27. Business owners should track their valuations as much as they do their current cash flow. (Chapter 28)

28. Some Business owners have to hit rock bottom in the selling process before they are willing to change their strategy. (Chapter 29)

29. An experienced M&A Advisor can assist a business owner with a team to equalize negotiations at the closing table. (Chapter 30)

30. The "Hosing at the Closing" scenario can and does happen. (Chapter 31)

31. A new "team-focused business-selling strategy" often produces a quality change in leadership style. (Chapter 32)

32. Executing the new plan will feel uncomfortable for the business owner at first, but then he will encounter, "Aha!" moments that build his confidence. (Chapter 33)

33. Not every employee will be on board with a new direction. (Chapter 34)

34. Business owners need to avoid the temptation to control every new process. (Chapter 35)

35. A team-oriented strategy often generates increased optimism and morale within the company culture. (Chapter 36)

36. Positive optimism and morale often reflect attractive financial statements. This is when it's time to sell the business. (Chapter 37)

37. Once a business sale is completed, the seller will reflect on his new purpose and obligations. (Chapter 38)

42
ACKNOWLEDGEMENTS

There are many I wish to thank who helped me in the creation of this book. First, thank you to my wife, Shannon, who managed our household and took care of our six kids while I spent many hours on this project. If it were not for her encouragement and enthusiasm this book never would have happened.

I also want to thank my friend Matt Kunz. He is an author, artist, and business professional, and without his guidance this book would still be just an idea. He helped turn it into a reality. For information about Matt Kunz, you can visit his website at www.mattkunz.com.

Thank you to those who contributed as beta readers. These are the ones who took the time to read Exit Teams and provided valuable feedback and guidance prior to its publication. I want to thank Steve Landrum, Robert Rosner, Brian Cochrum, and especially Pam Cravey. Pam analyzed every sentence and included pages full of detailed suggestions that went far beyond average. All of these beta readers gave tremendous insight, and for that I am grateful.

I also want to thank those who began reading Exit Teams and, though they were not able to provide their feedback before publication, have promised to put their reviews online,

BOB TANKESLEY, MBA, CPA

including Ben Nicholson, Buddy Turner, Scott Marmo, Bobby Wadley, Maria Forbes, and Brent Stromwall.

I also want to thank the over one hundred current and former business owner clients I have developed relationships with over the years. Our shared experiences have helped me grow so that, like them, more business owners could achieve the American Dream.

I also wish to thank my Grandparents Robert and Edna Tankesley. They were there for me when I needed them most, and without their help I would not have had the foundation and courage necessary to go after my dreams.

Finally, thanks to God above, for with Him all things are possible.

43
ABOUT THE AUTHOR

Bob Tankesley is a fourth-generation entrepreneur, serving as an M&A Advisor in the metro-Atlanta, GA region and beyond throughout the southeastern United States.

He has worked with owners of private businesses for over twenty-five years in various capacities, predominantly in the area of finance, but also for ten years specifically as an M&A Advisor.

He is a founding member of the Atlanta Chapter of XPX, a nationwide network of advisors to business owners working in a highly collaborative environment.

He has an undergraduate degree in accounting from U.N.C. Asheville and an M.B.A. in Finance from Appalachian State University.

Bob lives in Canton, GA. When he's not helping business owners, you can find him spending time with his wife and five kids on a trail somewhere above 3,000 feet in the Southeastern United States.

Made in the USA
Columbia, SC
20 September 2025